simply
Soup

simply
Soup

100 no fuss recipes for everyday cooking

First published in 2012
LOVE FOOD is an imprint of Parragon Books Ltd

Parragon
Queen Street House
4 Queen Street
Bath BA1 1HE, UK

www.parragon.com

ISBN: 978-1-4454-3764-4

Printed in China

Introduction by Linda Doeser
New recipes and cover food styling by Teresa Goldfinch
Cover photography by Clive Streeter
Additional photography by Clive Bozzard-Hill
Additional food styling by Valerie Barret

Notes for the Reader
This book uses standard kitchen measuring spoons and cups. All
spoon and cup measurements are level unless otherwise indicated.
Unless otherwise stated, milk is assumed to be whole, eggs are
large, individual vegetables are medium, and pepper is freshly
ground black pepper.

The times given are only an approximate guide. Preparation
times differ according to the techniques used by different people
and the cooking times may also vary from those given. Optional
ingredients, variations, or serving suggestions have not been
included in the calculations.

Recipes using raw or very lightly cooked eggs should be avoided
by infants, the elderly, pregnant women, convalescents, and anyone
with a chronic illness. Pregnant and breast-feeding women are
advised to avoid eating peanuts and peanut products. People with
nut allergies should be aware that some of the prepared ingredients
used in the recipes in this book may contain nuts. Always check the
packaging before use.

Contents

Introduction

There's something extra special about homemade soup. A meal-in-a-bowl broth with succulent chunks of meat or chicken or a tasty fish chowder is just the thing for a family lunch at the weekend. A refreshing chilled soup is an elegant appetizer for an al fresco lunch, while a silky textured bisque or crystal clear consommé is the perfect choice for the first course of a dinner party at any time of year. A warming rich and creamy soup is the ultimate comfort food after a bad day at work or when you're sniffing your way through a nasty head cold.

One of the great things about homemade soup—apart from its incomparable flavor—is that it's both quick and easy to make. After all, it's a one-pot dish that, once the initial preparation has been done, can be left to simmer gently to perfection until just before serving. It's also nutritious, immensely versatile, can be based on virtually every ingredient imaginable from meat, poultry, and fish to vegetables, fruit, and cheese, is easily adapted to suit family tastes, and can be as economical or luxurious as you like.

The basis for a really flavorsome soup is a good stock. Vegetable stocks are fairly quick to make but meat and poultry stocks are time-consuming. Fish stock will cook in about 30 minutes, but many people are unwilling to handle fish heads and trimmings. Fortunately, there are some excellent commercial stocks now available. While quite expensive, concentrated bottled stocks have the best flavor and do not usually include some of the less desirable additives, such as monosodium glutamate, found in some bouillon cubes. However, bouillon cubes and powders have improved tremendously in the last few years. Read the labels and avoid those with lots of additives or high levels of salt. Ready-made stocks from the chiller cabinet vary in quality, but price is usually a good indicator of what is worth buying.

You can make an easy vegetable stock by softening a diced onion, carrot, and celery stalk, plus any trimmings from such vegetables as fennel, mushrooms, leeks, broccoli, and asparagus, in 4 tablespoons of butter for 10 minutes. Add some fresh herb sprigs, pour in 3½ cups of water, and bring to a boil. Reduce the heat, partially cover the pan, and simmer for 15 minutes, then strain.

Top Tips for Success

• When preparing vegetables for soup, remember that they will be eaten with a spoon. Dice them finely enough to make this easy, although this is not a concern with soups that will be pureed at the end of cooking. Meat and poultry should also be cut into small cubes or thin strips.

• It is worth spending the time required to trim visible fat from meat to avoid unappetizing globules in the soup. If necessary, skim off any fat from the surface with a slotted spoon or blot up small amounts with paper towels. If it's very fatty, add a handful of ice cubes and when the fat has collected around them, scoop them out and discard.

• Like all dishes, soups are only as good as their ingredients. Carrots past their best, discolored cauliflower, and slimy onions will not be miraculously transformed in the pan.

• Once the soup mixture has come to a boil, reduce the heat, partially cover the pan, and simmer for the recommended time. Do not try to speed up the process by boiling the soup vigorously. Not only might it boil over, but there will be insufficient time for the flavors of the ingredients to mingle and blend.

• Go easy on seasoning, especially salt, during cooking since it may become so concentrated it spoils the flavor. If the soup is very salty, try adding a peeled potato, which will absorb some of the salt. Discard before serving.

• Remember to discard inedible flavorings, such as bay leaves, bouquets garnis, lemongrass stalks, and cinnamon sticks before serving—and before processing a creamy soup to a puree.

• Make the most of easy garnishes, such as chopped herbs, croutons, crumbled crisp-fried bacon, peeled and diced tomato, a swirl of cream, sour cream, or yogurt, grated Parmesan cheese, or even a spoonful of caviar or lumpfish roe. Try to match the garnish to the flavor of the soup.

• Make sure that soups to be served cold are well chilled and that hot soups really are steaming. Chilled or warmed soup bowls, as appropriate, are a good idea. A soup that has been processed in a food processor or blender will often need to be reheated gently before serving. If cream has been added at this stage, do not let the soup boil or it may curdle.

• Most soups freeze well and can be kept for up to 3 months. Do not add garnishes or embellishments, such as eggs or cream, to soups intended for freezing; add them on reheating.

1

Vegetable Plot

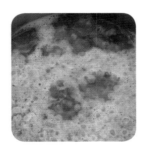

chunky vegetable soup

SERVES 6

2 carrots, sliced

1 onion, diced

1 garlic clove, crushed

12 oz/350 g new potatoes, diced

2 celery stalks, sliced

4 oz/115 g white mushrooms, quartered

14 oz/400 g canned chopped tomatoes

2½ cups vegetable stock

1 bay leaf

1 tsp dried mixed herbs or 1 tbsp chopped fresh mixed herbs

½ cup corn kernels, frozen or canned, drained

2 oz/55 g green cabbage, shredded

pepper

fresh basil sprigs, to garnish (optional)

1 Put the carrots, onion, garlic, potatoes, celery, mushrooms, tomatoes, and stock into a large saucepan. Stir in the bay leaf and herbs. Bring to a boil, then reduce the heat, cover, and let simmer for 25 minutes.

2 Add the corn and cabbage and return to a boil. Reduce the heat, cover, and simmer for 5 minutes, or until the vegetables are tender. Remove and discard the bay leaf. Season to taste with pepper.

3 Ladle into warmed bowls, garnish with basil, if using, and serve immediately.

minestrone

SERVES 4

2 tbsp olive oil

2 garlic cloves, chopped

2 red onions, chopped

1 red bell pepper, seeded and chopped

1 orange bell pepper, seeded and chopped

14 oz/400 g canned chopped tomatoes

4 cups vegetable stock

1 celery stalk, sliced

14 oz/400 g canned borlotti beans, drained

3½ oz/100 g green cabbage, shredded

2¾ oz/75 g frozen peas, thawed

1 tbsp chopped fresh parsley

2¾ oz/75 g dried vermicelli

salt and pepper

freshly grated Parmesan cheese, to garnish

1 Heat the oil in a large saucepan over medium heat, add the garlic and onions, and cook, stirring, for 3 minutes, until slightly softened. Add the red and orange bell peppers and the chopped tomatoes and cook for an additional 2 minutes, stirring. Stir in the stock, then add the celery, borlotti beans, cabbage, peas, and parsley. Season to taste with salt and pepper. Bring to a boil, then lower the heat and simmer for 30 minutes.

2 Add the vermicelli to the pan. Cook for another 10–12 minutes, or according to the directions on the package. Remove from the heat and ladle into warmed bowls. Garnish with freshly grated Parmesan cheese and serve immediately.

vegetable soup with pesto

SERVES 6

1 tbsp olive oil

1 onion, finely chopped

1 large leek, thinly sliced

1 celery stalk, thinly sliced

1 carrot, quartered and thinly sliced

1 garlic clove, finely chopped

6¼ cups water

1 potato, diced

1 parsnip, finely diced

1 small turnip, diced

5½ oz/150 g green beans, cut into small pieces

5½ oz/150 g fresh or frozen peas

2 small zucchini, quartered lengthwise and sliced

14 oz/400 g canned cannellini beans, drained and rinsed

3½ oz/100 g spinach leaves, cut into thin ribbons

1 tbsp basil pesto (in jar)

salt and pepper

fresh basil sprigs, to garnish (optional)

1 Heat the olive oil in a large saucepan over medium–low heat. Add the onion and leek and cook for 5 minutes, stirring occasionally, until the onion softens. Add the celery, carrot, and garlic and cook, covered, for an additional 5 minutes, stirring frequently.

2 Add the water, potato, parsnip, turnip, and green beans. Bring to a boil, reduce the heat to low, and simmer, covered, for 5 minutes.

3 Add the peas, zucchini, and cannellini beans and season to taste with salt and pepper. Cover again and simmer for about 25 minutes until all the vegetables are tender.

4 Add the spinach to the soup and simmer for an additional 5 minutes. Stir about a tablespoon of the pesto into the soup. Ladle into warmed bowls, garnish with basil, if using, and serve immediately.

potato & pea soup

SERVES 4

2 tbsp vegetable oil

8 oz/225 g starchy potatoes, diced

1 large onion, chopped

2 garlic cloves, crushed

1 tsp garam masala

1 tsp ground coriander

1 tsp ground cumin

3½ cups vegetable stock

1 fresh red chile, seeded and chopped

3½ oz/100 g frozen peas

4 tbsp plain yogurt

salt and pepper

chopped fresh cilantro, to garnish

1 Heat the oil in a large saucepan. Add the potatoes, onion, and garlic, and sauté over low heat, stirring constantly, for about 5 minutes. Add the garam masala, ground coriander, and cumin and cook, stirring constantly, for 1 minute.

2 Stir in the stock and red chile, and bring the mixture to a boil. Reduce the heat, cover the pan, and simmer for 20 minutes, until the potatoes begin to break down. Add the peas and cook for a further 5 minutes. Stir in the yogurt and season to taste with salt and pepper. Ladle into warmed bowls, garnish with chopped fresh cilantro, and serve immediately.

Step 1

Step 1

Step 3

tomato soup

SERVES 4

¼ cup butter

1 small onion, finely
chopped

1 lb/450 g tomatoes,
coarsely chopped

1 bay leaf

3 tbsp all-purpose flour

2½ cups milk

salt and pepper

fresh basil sprigs,
to garnish

1 Melt half the butter in a saucepan. Add the onion
and cook over low heat, stirring occasionally, for
5–6 minutes until softened. Add the tomatoes and bay leaf
and cook, stirring occasionally, for 15 minutes, or until pulpy.

2 Meanwhile, melt the remaining butter in another pan.
Add the flour and cook, stirring constantly, for 1 minute.
Remove the pan from the heat and gradually stir in the milk.
Return to the heat, season with salt and pepper, and bring
to a boil, stirring constantly. Continue to cook, stirring, until
smooth and thickened.

3 When the tomatoes are pulpy, remove the pan from the
heat. Discard the bay leaf and pour the tomato mixture
into a food processor or blender. Process until smooth, then
push through a fine strainer into a clean pan. Bring the
tomato puree to a boil, then gradually stir it into the milk
mixture. Season to taste with salt and pepper. Ladle into
warmed bowls, garnish with basil, and serve immediately.

french onion soup

SERVES 6

3 tbsp olive oil

1 lb 8 oz/675 g onions, thinly sliced

4 garlic cloves, 3 chopped and 1 halved

1 tsp sugar

2 tsp chopped fresh thyme, plus extra sprigs to garnish

2 tbsp all-purpose flour

½ cup dry white wine

8½ cups vegetable stock

6 slices French bread

10½ oz/300 g Gruyère cheese, grated

1 Heat the oil in a large, heavy saucepan over medium–low heat, add the onions, and cook, stirring occasionally, for 10 minutes, or until they are just beginning to brown. Stir in the chopped garlic, sugar, and chopped thyme, then reduce the heat and cook, stirring occasionally, for 30 minutes, or until the onions are golden brown.

2 Sprinkle in the flour and cook, stirring constantly, for 1–2 minutes. Stir in the wine. Gradually stir in the stock and bring to a boil, skimming off any foam that rises to the surface, then reduce the heat and simmer for 45 minutes.

3 Meanwhile, preheat the broiler to medium. Toast the bread on both sides under the broiler, then rub the toast with the cut edges of the halved garlic clove.

4 Ladle the soup into 6 ovenproof bowls set on a baking sheet. Float a piece of toast in each bowl and divide the grated cheese between them. Place under the broiler for 2–3 minutes, or until the cheese has just melted. Garnish with thyme sprigs and serve immediately.

creamy mushroom & tarragon soup

SERVES 4–6

3 tbsp butter

1 onion, chopped

1 lb 9 oz/700 g white mushrooms, coarsely chopped

3½ cups vegetable stock

3 tbsp chopped fresh tarragon, plus extra to garnish

⅔ cup sour cream

salt and pepper

1 Melt half the butter in a large saucepan. Add the onion and cook gently for 10 minutes, until soft. Add the remaining butter and the mushrooms and cook for 5 minutes, or until the mushrooms are browned.

2 Stir in the stock and tarragon, bring to a boil, then reduce the heat and simmer gently for 20 minutes. Transfer to a food processor or blender and process until smooth. Return the soup to the rinsed-out pan.

3 Stir in the sour cream and season to taste with salt and pepper. Reheat the soup gently until hot. Ladle into warmed bowls and garnish with chopped tarragon. Serve immediately.

spicy zucchini soup with rice

SERVES 4

2 tbsp vegetable oil

4 garlic cloves, thinly sliced

1–2 tbsp mild red chili powder

¼–½ tsp ground cumin

6 cups chicken, vegetable, or beef stock

2 zucchini, cut into bite-size chunks

4 tbsp long-grain rice

salt and pepper

fresh oregano sprigs, to garnish

lime wedges and crusty bread, to serve

1 Heat the oil in a heavy saucepan. Add the garlic and cook for 2 minutes, or until softened and just starting to change color. Add the chili powder and cumin and cook over medium–low heat for 1 minute.

2 Stir in the stock, zucchini, and rice, then cook over medium–high heat for 10 minutes, or until the zucchini are just tender and the rice is cooked through. Season to taste with salt and pepper.

3 Ladle into warmed bowls, then garnish with oregano sprigs and serve immediately with lime wedges and crusty bread.

Step 1

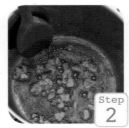

Step 2

Step 2

tuscan bean soup

SERVES 6

**10½ oz/300 g canned
cannellini beans,
drained and rinsed**

**10½ oz/300 g canned
cranberry beans,
drained and rinsed**

2½ cups vegetable stock

**4 oz/115 g dried
conchigliette or other
small pasta shapes**

4 tbsp olive oil

**2 garlic cloves, very finely
chopped**

**3 tbsp chopped fresh
flat-leaf parsley**

salt and pepper

1 Place half the cannellini and half the cranberry beans in a food processor or blender with half the stock and process until smooth. Pour into a large, heavy saucepan and add the remaining beans. Stir in enough of the remaining stock to achieve the consistency you like, then bring to a boil.

2 Add the pasta and return to a boil, then reduce the heat and cook for 15 minutes, or until just tender.

3 Meanwhile, heat 3 tablespoons of the oil in a small skillet. Add the garlic and cook, stirring constantly, for 2–3 minutes, or until golden. Stir the garlic into the soup with the parsley.

4 Season to taste with salt and pepper and ladle into warmed bowls. Drizzle with the remaining olive oil and serve immediately.

cauliflower soup

SERVES 6

1 tbsp olive oil

2 tbsp butter

1 large onion, coarsely chopped

2 leeks, sliced

1 large head of cauliflower

3¾ cups vegetable stock

salt and pepper

finely grated Cheddar cheese and extra virgin olive oil, to serve

1 Heat the oil and butter in a large saucepan and cook the onion and leeks for 10 minutes, stirring frequently, taking care not to allow the vegetables to color.

2 Cut the cauliflower into florets and cut the stalk into small pieces. Add to the pan and sauté with the other vegetables for 2–3 minutes.

3 Add the stock and bring to a boil, cover, and simmer over medium heat for 20 minutes.

4 Pour the soup into a food processor or blender, process until smooth, and return to the rinsed-out saucepan.

5 Heat the soup through, season to taste with salt and pepper, and serve immediately in warmed bowls garnished with a spoonful of grated cheese and a drizzle of extra virgin olive oil.

creamy carrot & parsnip soup

SERVES 4

4 tbsp butter
1 large onion, chopped
1 lb/450 g carrots, chopped
2 large parsnips, chopped
1 tbsp grated fresh ginger
1 tsp grated orange zest
2½ cups vegetable stock
½ cup light cream
salt and pepper
fresh cilantro sprigs,
to garnish

1 Melt the butter in a large saucepan over low heat. Add the onion and cook, stirring, for 3 minutes, until slightly softened. Add the carrots and parsnips, cover the pan, and cook, stirring occasionally, for about 15 minutes, until the vegetables have softened a little. Stir in the ginger, orange zest, and stock. Bring to a boil, then reduce the heat, cover the pan, and simmer for 30–35 minutes, until the vegetables are tender. Remove the soup from the heat and let cool for 10 minutes.

2 Transfer the soup to a food processor or blender and process until smooth. Return the soup to the rinsed-out pan, stir in the cream, and season to taste with salt and pepper. Warm through gently over low heat.

3 Remove from the heat and ladle into warmed bowls. Garnish with pepper and cilantro sprigs and serve immediately.

butternut squash & bacon soup

SERVES 4

2 tbsp olive oil

5 bacon strips, chopped

1 large onion, coarsely chopped

2 celery stalks, coarsely chopped

2 tsp chopped fresh thyme leaves

1 lb 7 oz/650 g butternut squash, peeled, seeded, and cut into chunks

1 large red bell pepper, seeded and coarsely chopped

2½ cups vegetable stock

½ tsp smoked paprika

crispy broiled bacon and toasted pumpkin seeds, to garnish

1 Heat the oil in a large saucepan over low heat. Add the bacon and cook until the fat from the bacon starts to run. Stir in the onion, celery, and thyme. Cover and cook for 10 minutes, until the onion looks translucent.

2 Stir in the squash, bell pepper, stock, and smoked paprika. Bring to a boil, then reduce the heat, cover, and simmer for 30 minutes, until the vegetables are tender. Remove from the heat and let cool slightly.

3 Transfer the soup to a food processor or blender and process until smooth. Return to the rinsed-out pan and heat through. Remove from the heat and ladle into warmed mugs. Garnish with crispy broiled bacon and toasted pumpkin seeds, and serve immediately.

Step 1

Step 2

Step 3

spiced pumpkin soup

SERVES 4

2 tbsp olive oil

1 onion, chopped

1 garlic clove, chopped

1 tbsp chopped fresh ginger

1 small fresh red chile, seeded and finely chopped

2 tbsp chopped fresh cilantro

1 bay leaf

2 lb 4 oz/1 kg pumpkin, peeled, seeded, and diced

2½ cups vegetable stock

salt and pepper

light cream, to garnish

1 Heat the oil in a saucepan over medium heat. Add the onion and garlic and cook, stirring, for about 4 minutes, until slightly softened. Add the ginger, chile, cilantro, bay leaf, and pumpkin, and cook for another 3 minutes.

2 Pour in the stock and bring to a boil, skimming off any foam that rises to the surface. Reduce the heat and simmer gently, stirring occasionally, for about 25 minutes, or until the pumpkin is tender. Remove from the heat, remove and discard the bay leaf, and let cool a little.

3 Transfer the soup to a food processor or blender and process until smooth. Return the mixture to the rinsed-out pan and season to taste with salt and pepper. Reheat gently, stirring. Remove from the heat and ladle into warmed bowls. Garnish with a swirl of cream, and serve immediately.

roasted squash & sweet potato soup

SERVES 6–8

1 sweet potato, about 12 oz/350 g

1 acorn squash

4 shallots

2 tbsp olive oil

5–6 garlic cloves, unpeeled

3¾ cups vegetable stock

½ cup light cream

salt and pepper

chopped fresh chives, to garnish

1 Preheat the oven to 375°F/190°C. Cut the sweet potato, squash, and shallots in half lengthwise, through to the stem end. Scoop the seeds out of the squash. Brush the cut sides with the oil.

2 Put the vegetables, cut-side down, in a shallow roasting pan. Add the garlic cloves and roast in the preheated oven for about 40 minutes, until tender and light brown.

3 When cool, scoop the flesh from the potato and squash halves, and put in a saucepan with the shallots. Remove the garlic peel and add the soft insides to the other vegetables.

4 Add the stock and a pinch of salt. Bring just to a boil, reduce the heat, and simmer, partially covered, for about 30 minutes, stirring occasionally, until the vegetables are very tender.

5 Allow the soup to cool, then transfer to a food processor or blender and process until smooth.

6 Return the soup to the rinsed-out pan and stir in the cream. Season to taste with salt and pepper, and reheat. Ladle into warmed bowls, garnish with chives, and serve immediately.

curried zucchini soup

SERVES 4

2 tsp butter

1 large onion, finely chopped

2 lb/900 g zucchini, sliced

2 cups chicken or vegetable stock

1 tsp curry powder

½ cup sour cream, plus extra to garnish

salt and pepper

1 Melt the butter in a large saucepan over medium heat. Add the onion and cook for about 3 minutes, or until it begins to soften.

2 Add the zucchini, stock, and curry powder, along with a large pinch of salt, if using unsalted stock. Bring the soup to a boil, reduce the heat, cover, and cook gently for about 25 minutes, or until the vegetables are tender.

3 Allow the soup to cool slightly, then transfer to a food processor or blender and process until smooth, but still green with flecks. (If using a food processor, strain off the cooking liquid and reserve. Process the soup solids with enough cooking liquid to moisten them, then combine with the remaining liquid.)

4 Return the soup to the rinsed-out saucepan and stir in the sour cream. Reheat gently over low heat. Do not boil.

5 Ladle into warmed bowls, garnish with a swirl of sour cream, and serve immediately.

leek & potato soup

SERVES 4–6

¼ cup butter

1 onion, chopped

3 leeks, sliced

8 oz/225 g potatoes, cut into ¾-inch/2-cm cubes

3½ cups vegetable stock

salt and pepper

2 tbsp chopped fresh chives, to garnish

⅔ cup light cream (optional) and crusty bread, to serve

1 Melt the butter in a large saucepan over medium heat, add the onion, leeks, and potatoes, and sauté gently for 2–3 minutes, until softened but not browned. Pour in the stock, bring to a boil, then reduce the heat and simmer, covered, for 15 minutes.

2 Transfer the mixture to a food processor or blender and process until smooth. Return to the rinsed-out saucepan.

3 Heat the soup gently and season to taste with salt and pepper. Remove from the heat and ladle into warmed bowls. Swirl with the cream, garnish with chives, and serve immediately with crusty bread.

Step 1

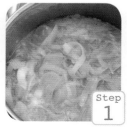
Step 1

Step 2

Vea
p'

sweet potato & blue cheese soup

SERVES 4

4 tbsp butter

1 large onion, chopped

2 leeks, sliced

6 oz/175 g sweet potatoes, peeled and diced

3½ cups vegetable stock

1 tbsp chopped fresh parsley

1 bay leaf

⅔ cup heavy cream

5½ oz/150 g blue cheese, crumbled

pepper

2 tbsp finely crumbled blue cheese, to garnish

thick slices fresh bread, to serve

1 Melt the butter in a large saucepan over medium heat. Add the onion and leeks and cook, stirring, for about 3 minutes, until slightly softened. Add the sweet potatoes and cook for another 5 minutes, stirring, then pour in the stock, add the parsley and the bay leaf, and season to taste with pepper. Bring to a boil, then lower the heat, cover the pan, and simmer for about 30 minutes. Remove from the heat and let cool for 10 minutes. Remove and discard the bay leaf.

2 Transfer half of the soup into a food processor or blender and process until smooth. Return the soup to the rinsed-out pan with the rest of the soup, stir in the cream, and cook for another 5 minutes. Gradually stir in the crumbled cheese until melted. Do not boil.

3 Remove from the heat and ladle into warmed bowls. Garnish with finely crumbled cheese and serve immediately with slices of fresh bread.

watercress soup

SERVES 4

**2 bunches watercress
(about 7 oz/200 g)**

3 tbsp butter

2 onions, chopped

**8 oz/225 g potatoes,
coarsely chopped**

**5 cups vegetable stock or
water**

salt and pepper

**whole nutmeg (optional)
and ½ cup sour cream or
plain yogurt, to garnish**

1 Remove the leaves from the stalks of the watercress and set aside. Coarsely chop the stalks.

2 Melt the butter in a large saucepan over medium heat, add the onions, and cook for 4–5 minutes, until soft. Do not brown.

3 Add the potatoes to the saucepan and mix well with the onions. Add the watercress stalks and the stock.

4 Bring to a boil, then reduce the heat, cover, and simmer for 15–20 minutes, until the potatoes are soft.

5 Add the watercress leaves and stir in to heat through. Remove from the heat and transfer to a food processor or blender and process until smooth. Return the soup to the rinsed-out saucepan. Reheat and season to taste with salt and pepper, adding a good grating of nutmeg, if using.

6 Serve immediately in warmed bowls with the sour cream spooned on top and an extra grating of nutmeg, if desired.

cream of pea soup

SERVES 4

4 tbsp butter

1 onion, finely chopped

1 lb/450 g shelled peas

½ cup water

2½–3 cups milk

salt and pepper

1 Melt the butter in a saucepan over low heat. Add the onion and cook, stirring occasionally, for 5 minutes until softened.

2 Add the peas and pour in the water. Increase the heat to medium and simmer for 3–4 minutes, or until the peas are tender. (Frozen peas will be ready in 10 minutes.)

3 Add 2½ cups of the milk, season to taste with salt and pepper, and bring to a boil, stirring continuously.

4 Remove the pan from the heat and let cool slightly, then pour the soup into a food processor or blender and process until smooth.

5 Return the soup to the rinsed-out pan and bring back to a boil. (If the soup seems too thick, heat the remaining milk in a small pan and stir it into the soup.) Remove from the heat, ladle into warmed bowls, and serve immediately.

pea & bean soup

SERVES 4–6

1½ tbsp olive oil

1 bunch scallions, chopped

1 large celery stalk, chopped

1 garlic clove, crushed

1 starchy potato, about 5½ oz/150 g, peeled and diced

5 cups vegetable stock

1 bay leaf

5½ oz/150 g peas

14 oz/400 g canned flageolets, drained and rinsed

salt and pepper

finely shredded fresh mint, to garnish

mixed-grain bread rolls, to serve

1 Heat the oil in a large saucepan over medium–high heat. Add the scallions, celery, and garlic and cook, stirring, for about 3 minutes, or until softened. Add the potato and stir for an additional minute.

2 Add the stock and bay leaf. Season to taste with salt and pepper and bring to a boil, stirring. Reduce the heat to low, cover the pan, and simmer for 20 minutes, or until the potatoes are tender.

3 Add the peas and flageolets and return the soup to a boil. Reduce the heat, re-cover the pan, and continue to simmer until the peas are tender.

4 Remove and discard the bay leaf, then transfer the soup to a food processor or blender and process until smooth. Place a metal strainer over the rinsed-out pan and use a wooden spoon to push the soup through the strainer.

5 Reheat gently and season to taste with salt and pepper. Remove from the heat and ladle into warmed bowls. Sprinkle with mint, and serve immediately with bread rolls.

Step 1

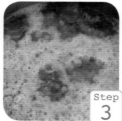
Step 3

Step 4

spinach & cheese soup

SERVES 6–8

8 oz/225 g fresh baby spinach leaves, tough stalks removed

2½ cups milk

3 cups vegetable stock

scant 1 cup cream cheese flavored with garlic and herbs

salt and pepper

croutons (optional)

1 Put the spinach in a large saucepan and pour in the milk and stock. Bring to a boil, then reduce the heat and simmer gently for 12 minutes. Remove the pan from the heat and let cool completely.

2 Ladle the cold soup into a food processor or blender and process until smooth. Cut the cheese into chunks and add to the soup. Process again until smooth and creamy.

3 Pour the soup into a large bowl and season with salt and pepper to taste. Cover with plastic wrap and let chill in the refrigerator for at least 3 hours. Stir well before ladling into chilled bowls. Add croutons, if using, and serve immediately.

gazpacho

SERVES 4

**9 oz/250 g white bread
slices, crusts removed**

**1 lb 9 oz/700 g tomatoes,
peeled and chopped**

**3 garlic cloves, coarsely
chopped**

**2 red bell peppers, seeded
and chopped**

**1 cucumber, peeled,
seeded, and chopped**

5 tbsp extra virgin olive oil

5 tbsp red wine vinegar

1 tbsp tomato paste

9½ cups water

salt and pepper

4 ice cubes, to serve

1 Tear the bread into pieces and place in a blender. Process briefly to make breadcrumbs and transfer to a large bowl. Add the tomatoes, garlic, bell peppers, cucumber, olive oil, vinegar, and tomato paste. Mix well.

2 Working in batches, place the tomato mixture with about the same amount of the measured water in the food processor or blender and process until smooth. Transfer to another bowl. When all the tomato mixture and water have been blended together, stir well and season to taste with salt and pepper. Cover with plastic wrap and chill in the refrigerator for at least 2 hours, but no longer than 12 hours.

3 When ready to serve, ladle the soup into chilled bowls and float an ice cube in each bowl. Serve immediately.

chilled pepper & orange soup

SERVES 4

5 blood oranges

3 tbsp olive oil

3 lb 5 oz/1.5 kg red bell peppers, seeded and sliced

1½ tbsp orange flower water

salt and pepper

extra virgin olive oil, for drizzling (optional)

1 Finely grate the rind of one of the oranges and shred the rind of another with a citrus zester. Set aside. Squeeze the juice from all the oranges.

2 Heat the oil in a saucepan, add the red bell peppers, and cook over medium heat, stirring occasionally, for 10 minutes. Stir in the grated orange rind and cook for an additional few minutes. Reduce the heat, cover, and simmer gently, stirring occasionally, for 20 minutes.

3 Remove the pan from the heat, let cool slightly, then transfer the red pepper mixture to a food processor or blender and process until smooth. Add the orange juice and orange flower water and process again until thoroughly combined.

4 Transfer the soup to a large bowl, season with salt and pepper to taste, and let cool completely, then cover with plastic wrap and chill in the refrigerator for 3 hours. Stir well and ladle into chilled bowls. Serve immediately, sprinkled with the shredded orange rind and drizzled with olive oil, if using.

chilled garlic soup

SERVES 4–6

1 lb 2 oz/500 g day-old Italian or French white bread, crusts removed, then torn

5 large garlic cloves, halved

½ cup extra virgin olive oil, plus a little extra, to garnish

4–5 tbsp sherry vinegar, to taste

generous 3 cups ground almonds

5 cups water, chilled

seedless white grapes, to garnish

1 Put the bread in a bowl with just enough cold water to cover and soak for 15 minutes. Squeeze the bread dry and transfer it to a food processor or blender.

2 Add the garlic, oil, 4 tablespoons of sherry vinegar, and the ground almonds to the food processor with 1 cup of the water and process until blended.

3 With the motor running, slowly pour in the remaining water and process until smooth. Transfer the soup to a large bowl and add extra sherry vinegar, if necessary. Cover with plastic wrap and chill in the refrigerator for at least 4 hours.

4 Ladle into chilled bowls and garnish with grapes and a drizzle of olive oil. Serve immediately.

VARIATION

For something slightly different, replace the sherry vinegar with 4 tablespoons of dry sherry.

Fabulous Fish & Seafood

mixed fish soup

SERVES 4

1 tbsp butter

2 shallots, chopped

1 leek, sliced

3 tbsp all-purpose flour

generous 2 cups fish stock

1 bay leaf

generous 2 cups milk

2 tbsp dry sherry

2 tbsp lemon juice

1 lb 5 oz/600 g various whitefish fillets, skinned

7 oz/200 g canned or freshly cooked crabmeat

5½ oz/150 g canned corn kernels, drained

generous ¾ cup heavy cream

salt and pepper

fresh dill sprigs and lemon wedges, to garnish

1 Melt the butter in a large saucepan over medium heat. Add the shallots and leek and cook, stirring, for about 3 minutes, until slightly softened. In a bowl, mix the flour with enough stock to make a smooth paste, then stir it into the pan. Cook, stirring, for 2 minutes, then gradually stir in the remaining stock. Add the bay leaf and season to taste with salt and pepper. Bring to a boil, then lower the heat. Pour in the milk and sherry and stir in the lemon juice. Simmer for 15 minutes.

2 Rinse the fish under cold running water, then drain and cut into bite-size chunks. Add to the soup with the crabmeat and corn. Cook for 15 minutes, until the fish is tender and cooked through. Stir in the cream. Cook for another 2–3 minutes, then remove from the heat and remove and discard the bay leaf.

3 Ladle into warmed bowls, garnish with sprigs of fresh dill and lemon wedges, and serve immediately.

tuna chowder

SERVES 4

2 tbsp butter

1 large garlic clove, chopped

1 large onion, sliced

1 carrot, chopped

2½ cups fish stock

14 oz/400 g potatoes, peeled and cut into bite-size chunks

14 oz/400 g canned chopped tomatoes

14 oz/400 g canned cannellini beans, drained

1 tbsp tomato paste

1 zucchini, chopped

8 oz/225 g canned tuna in brine, drained

1 tbsp chopped fresh basil

1 tbsp chopped fresh parsley

scant ½ cup heavy cream

salt and pepper

fresh basil sprigs, to garnish

1 Melt the butter in a large saucepan over low heat. Add the garlic and onion and cook, stirring, for 3 minutes, until slightly softened. Add the carrot and cook for another 5 minutes, stirring. Pour in the stock, then add the potatoes, tomatoes, beans, and tomato paste. Season to taste with salt and pepper. Bring to a boil, then reduce the heat, cover the pan, and simmer for 20 minutes.

2 Add the zucchini, tuna, and chopped basil and parsley and cook for another 15 minutes. Stir in the cream and cook the soup very gently for another 2 minutes.

3 Remove from the heat and ladle into warmed bowls. Garnish with sprigs of fresh basil, and serve immediately.

genoese fish soup

SERVES 4

2 tbsp butter

1 onion, chopped

1 garlic clove, finely chopped

2 oz/55 g bacon, diced

2 celery stalks, chopped

14 oz/400 g canned chopped tomatoes

⅔ cup dry white wine

1¼ cups fish stock

4 fresh basil leaves, torn

2 tbsp chopped fresh flat-leaf parsley

1 lb/450 g whitefish fillets, such as cod or monkfish, skinned and chopped

4 oz/115 g cooked peeled shrimp

salt and pepper

1 Melt the butter in a large, heavy saucepan. Add the onion and garlic and cook over low heat, stirring occasionally, for 5 minutes, or until softened.

2 Add the bacon and celery and cook, stirring frequently, for an additional 2 minutes.

3 Add the tomatoes, wine, stock, basil, and 1 tablespoon of the parsley. Season to taste with salt and pepper. Bring to a boil, then reduce the heat and simmer for 10 minutes.

4 Add the fish and cook for 5 minutes, or until it is opaque. Add the shrimp and heat through gently for 3 minutes. Ladle into warmed bowls, garnish with the remaining chopped parsley, and serve immediately.

hot & sour soup with salmon

SERVES 4

8 oz/225 g skinless salmon fillet, cut into 2–3 pieces

2 tsp sesame oil

4 cups chicken or vegetable stock

1 oz/25 g fresh cilantro, stalks and leaves separated

2 Thai chiles, halved lengthwise

1 lemongrass stalk, coarsely chopped

3¼ cups cremini mushrooms, quartered

2 tbsp Thai fish sauce

1½ cups snow peas, diagonally sliced

4 scallions, thinly sliced

finely grated zest and juice of 2 limes

1 Preheat the broiler to high. Put the salmon on an aluminum foil-lined broiler pan and brush lightly with the sesame oil. Broil for 3–4 minutes, until just cooked through. Flake into bite-size pieces and set aside.

2 Pour the stock into a large saucepan. Add the cilantro stalks, chiles, and lemongrass. Bring to a boil, cover, and simmer for 5 minutes. Strain into a bowl, discard the flavorings, and return the stock to the pan.

3 Add the mushrooms and Thai fish sauce to the pan. Cover and simmer for 3 minutes. Meanwhile shred half the cilantro leaves.

4 Add the snow peas, scallions, shredded cilantro leaves, salmon, and lime zest to the pan and gently heat through. Stir in all the lime juice or add to taste. Remove from the heat and ladle into warmed bowls. Sprinkle with the remaining cilantro leaves and serve immediately.

Step 1

Step 2

Step 3

bouillabaisse

SERVES 4

scant ½ cup olive oil

3 garlic cloves, chopped

2 onions, chopped

2 tomatoes, seeded and chopped

2¾ cups fish stock

1¾ cups white wine

1 bay leaf

pinch of saffron threads

2 tbsp chopped fresh basil

2 tbsp chopped fresh parsley

7 oz/200 g mussels

9 oz/250 g snapper or monkfish fillets

9 oz/250 g whitefish fillets, skinned

7 oz/200 g shrimp, peeled and deveined

3½ oz/100 g scallops

salt and pepper

1 Heat the oil in a large saucepan over medium heat. Add the garlic and onions and cook, stirring, for 3 minutes. Stir in the tomatoes, stock, wine, bay leaf, saffron, and herbs. Bring to a boil, reduce the heat, cover, and simmer for 30 minutes.

2 Meanwhile, soak the mussels in lightly salted water for 10 minutes. Scrub the shells under cold running water and pull off any beards. Discard any mussels with broken shells or any that refuse to close when tapped. Put the rest into a large pan with a little water, bring to a boil, and cook over high heat for 4 minutes, or until the mussels open. Remove from the heat and discard any that remain closed.

3 When the tomato mixture is cooked, rinse the fish, pat dry, and cut into chunks. Add to the pan and simmer for 5 minutes. Add the mussels, shrimp, and scallops and season to taste with salt and pepper. Cook for 3 minutes, until the fish is cooked through. Remove from the heat, remove and discard the bay leaf, and ladle into warmed bowls. Serve immediately.

thai-style seafood soup

SERVES 4

5 cups fish stock

1 lemongrass stalk, split lengthwise

pared rind of ½ lime, or 1 lime leaf

1-inch/2.5-cm piece fresh ginger, sliced

¼ tsp chili paste, or to taste

7 oz/200 g large or medium raw shrimp, peeled and deveined

4–6 scallions, sliced

9 oz/250 g scallops

2 tbsp fresh cilantro leaves

salt

finely sliced red chiles, to garnish

1 Put the stock in a saucepan with the lemongrass, lime rind, ginger, and chili paste. Bring just to a boil, reduce the heat, cover, and simmer for 10–15 minutes.

2 Cut the shrimp almost in half lengthwise, keeping the tail intact.

3 Strain the stock, return to the saucepan, and bring to a simmer. Add the scallions and cook for 2–3 minutes. Taste and season to taste with salt, if needed, and stir in a little more chili paste, if desired.

4 Add the scallops and shrimp and poach for about 1 minute until they turn opaque and the shrimp curl.

5 Stir in the fresh cilantro leaves. Remove from the heat and ladle the soup into warmed bowls, dividing the shellfish evenly. Garnish with chiles and serve immediately.

seared scallops in garlic broth

SERVES 4

**1 large garlic bulb
(about 3½ oz/100 g),
separated into unpeeled
cloves**

1 celery stalk, chopped

1 carrot, chopped

1 onion, chopped

10 peppercorns

5–6 parsley stems

5 cups water

8 oz/225 g large scallops

1 tbsp oil

salt and pepper

**fresh cilantro leaves,
to garnish**

1 Combine the garlic cloves, celery, carrot, onion, peppercorns, parsley stems, and water in a saucepan with a good pinch of salt. Bring to a boil, reduce the heat, and simmer, partially covered, for 30–45 minutes.

2 Strain the stock into a clean saucepan and keep hot. Slice each scallop in half to form 2 thinner rounds. (If the scallops are very large, slice them into 3 rounds.) Sprinkle with salt and pepper.

3 Heat the oil in a skillet over medium–high heat and cook the scallops on one side for 1–2 minutes, until lightly browned and the flesh becomes opaque.

4 Remove from the heat and divide the scallops between warmed bowls. Ladle over the stock, garnish with cilantro and serve immediately.

squid, chorizo & tomato soup

SERVES 6

1 lb/450 g cleaned squid

5½ oz/150 g lean chorizo, peeled and very finely diced

1 onion, finely chopped

1 celery stalk, thinly sliced

1 carrot, thinly sliced

2 garlic cloves, finely chopped or crushed

14 oz/400 g canned chopped tomatoes

5 cups fish stock

½ tsp ground cumin

pinch of saffron

1 bay leaf

chili paste (optional)

salt and pepper

fresh chopped parsley, to garnish

1 Cut off the squid tentacles and cut into bite-sized pieces. Slice the bodies into rings.

2 Place a large saucepan over medium–low heat and add the chorizo. Cook for 5–10 minutes, stirring frequently, until it renders most of its fat. Remove with a slotted spoon and drain on paper towels.

3 Pour off all the fat from the pan and add the onion, celery, carrot, and garlic. Cover and cook for 3–4 minutes, until the onion is slightly softened.

4 Stir in the tomatoes, fish stock, cumin, saffron, bay leaf, and chorizo.

5 Add the squid to the soup. Bring almost to a boil, reduce the heat, cover, and cook gently for 40–45 minutes, or until the squid and carrot are tender, stirring occasionally. Remove and discard the bay leaf.

6 Stir in a little chili paste, if using, for a spicier flavor, and season to taste with salt and pepper. Ladle into warmed bowls, garnish with parsley, and serve immediately.

Step 1

Step 2

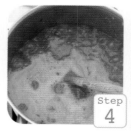
Step 4

saffron mussel soup

SERVES 4–6

4 lb 8 oz/2 kg mussels

⅔ cup dry white wine

1 tbsp butter

2 large shallots, finely chopped

1 leek, halved lengthwise and thinly sliced

pinch of saffron threads

1¼ cups heavy cream

1 tbsp cornstarch, dissolved in 2 tbsp water

2 tbsp chopped fresh parsley

salt and pepper

1 Scrub the mussels under cold running water and pull off any beards. Discard any mussels with broken shells or any that refuse to close when tapped.

2 Put the mussels in a large, heavy saucepan over high heat with the wine and a little pepper. Cover tightly and cook for 4–5 minutes, or until the mussels open, shaking the pan occasionally. Discard any that remain closed.

3 When they are cool enough to handle, remove the mussels from the shells, adding any additional juices to the cooking liquid. Strain the cooking liquid through a cheesecloth-lined sieve. Top up the cooking liquid with water to make 4 cups.

4 Melt the butter in a heavy saucepan. Add the shallots and leek, cover, and cook until they begin to soften, stirring occasionally.

5 Stir in the mussel cooking liquid and the saffron and season to taste with salt and pepper. Bring to a boil, reduce the heat, and simmer for 15–20 minutes, or until the vegetables are very tender.

6 Add the cream, stir, and bring just to a boil. Stir the dissolved cornstarch into the soup and boil gently for 2–3 minutes, until slightly thickened, stirring frequently. Add the mussels and cook for 1–2 minutes to reheat them. Remove from the heat and stir in the parsley. Ladle into warmed bowls, and serve immediately.

clam & corn chowder

SERVES 4

1 lb 10 oz/750 g clams, or 10 oz/280 g canned clams

2 tbsp dry white wine (if using fresh clams)

4 tsp butter

1 large onion, finely chopped

1 small carrot, finely diced

3 tbsp all-purpose flour

1¼ cups fish stock

¾ cup water (if using canned clams)

1 lb/450 g potatoes, diced

1 cup corn, thawed if frozen

2 cups whole milk

salt and pepper

chopped fresh parsley, to garnish

1 If using fresh clams, wash under cold running water. Discard any with broken shells or any that refuse to close when tapped. Put the clams into a heavy saucepan with the wine. Cover tightly, set over medium–high heat, and cook for 2–4 minutes, or until they open, shaking the pan occasionally. Discard any that remain closed. Remove the clams from the shells and strain the cooking liquid through a cheesecloth-lined strainer; reserve both. If using canned clams, drain and rinse well.

2 Melt the butter in a large pan over medium–low heat. Add the onion and carrot and cook for 3–4 minutes, stirring frequently, until the onion is softened. Stir in the flour and continue cooking for 2 minutes.

3 Slowly add about half the stock and stir well, scraping the bottom of the pan to mix in the flour. Pour in the remaining stock and the reserved clam cooking liquid, or the water if using canned clams, and bring just to a boil, stirring.

4 Add the potatoes, corn, and milk and stir to combine. Reduce the heat, season to taste with salt and pepper, and simmer gently, partially covered, for about 20 minutes, stirring occasionally, until all the vegetables are tender.

5 Chop the clams, if large. Stir in the clams and continue cooking for about 5 minutes until heated through. Remove from the heat and ladle into warmed bowls. Garnish with parsley and serve immediately.

creamy oyster soup

SERVES 4

12 oysters

1 tbsp butter

2 shallots, finely chopped

5 tbsp white wine

1¼ cups fish stock

¾ cup heavy cream

2 tbsp cornstarch, dissolved in 2 tbsp cold water

salt and pepper

caviar or lumpfish roe, to garnish (optional)

1 To open the oysters, hold flat-side up, over a strainer set over a bowl to catch the juices, and push an oyster knife into the hinge. Work it around until you can pry off the top shell. When all the oysters have been opened, strain the liquid through a cheesecloth-lined sieve. Remove any bits of shell stuck to the oysters and reserve them in their liquid.

2 Melt the butter in a saucepan over low heat. Add the shallots and cook gently for about 5 minutes, until just softened, stirring frequently; do not allow them to brown.

3 Add the wine, bring to a boil, and boil for 1 minute. Stir in the fish stock, bring back to a boil, and boil for 3–4 minutes. Reduce the heat to a gentle simmer.

4 Add the oysters and their liquid and poach for about 1 minute, until they become firmer but are still tender. Remove the oysters with a slotted spoon and reserve, covered. Strain the stock.

5 Bring the strained stock to a boil in a clean saucepan. Add the cream and bring back to a boil.

6 Stir the dissolved cornstarch into the soup and boil gently for 2–3 minutes, stirring frequently, until slightly thickened. Add the oysters and cook for 1–2 minutes to reheat them. Ladle the soup into warmed bowls. Garnish each serving with a teaspoon of caviar, if using, and serve immediately.

fisherman's soup

SERVES 6

2 lb/900 g mixed white fish fillets and shellfish, such as cod, flounder, halibut, monkfish, sea bass, whiting, and peeled shrimp

⅔ cup olive oil

2 large onions, sliced

2 celery stalks, sliced thinly

2 garlic cloves, chopped

⅔ cup white wine

4 canned tomatoes, chopped

pared rind of 1 orange

1 tsp chopped fresh thyme

2 tbsp chopped fresh parsley

2 bay leaves

salt and pepper

lemon wedges and croutons, to serve

1 Cut the fish into fairly large, thick, serving portions, discarding any skin. Heat the oil in a large saucepan, add the onions, celery, and garlic and fry for 5 minutes, until softened.

2 Add the fish and shrimp to the pan then add the wine, tomatoes, pared orange rind, thyme, parsley, and bay leaves. Season to taste with salt and pepper, and add enough cold water to cover. Bring to a boil then simmer, uncovered, for 15 minutes.

3 Remove from the heat and remove and discard the bay leaves. Ladle into warmed bowls and serve immediately, with lemon wedges, and croutons.

Step
1

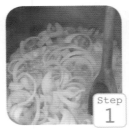

Step
1

Step
2

shrimp & vegetable bisque

SERVES 4

3 tbsp butter

1 garlic clove, chopped

1 onion, sliced

1 carrot, chopped

1 celery stalk, sliced

5 cups fish stock

4 tbsp red wine

1 tbsp tomato paste

1 bay leaf

1 lb 5 oz/600 g shrimp, peeled and deveined

scant ½ cup heavy cream

salt and pepper

light cream and whole cooked shrimp, to garnish

1 Melt the butter in a large saucepan over medium heat. Add the garlic and onion and cook, stirring, for 3 minutes, until slightly softened. Add the carrot and celery and cook for another 3 minutes, stirring. Pour in the stock and red wine, then add the tomato paste and bay leaf. Season to taste with salt and pepper. Bring to a boil, then lower the heat and simmer for 20 minutes. Remove from the heat and let cool for 10 minutes, then remove and discard the bay leaf.

2 Transfer half of the soup to a food processor or blender and process until smooth. Return to the pan with the rest of the soup. Add the shrimp and cook the soup over low heat for 5–6 minutes.

3 Stir in the heavy cream and cook for another 2 minutes, then remove from the heat and ladle into warmed bowls. Garnish with swirls of light cream and whole cooked shrimp, and serve immediately.

fennel & tomato soup with shrimp

SERVES 4

2 tsp olive oil

1 large onion, halved and sliced

2 large fennel bulbs, halved and sliced

1 small potato, diced

3¾ cups water

1⅔ cups tomato juice, plus extra if needed

1 bay leaf

4½ oz/125 g cooked peeled small shrimp

2 tomatoes, skinned, seeded, and chopped

½ tsp snipped fresh dill

salt and pepper

dill sprigs or fennel fronds, to garnish

1 Heat the olive oil in a large saucepan over medium heat. Add the onion and fennel and cook for 3–4 minutes, stirring occasionally, until the onion is just softened.

2 Add the potato, water, tomato juice, and bay leaf with a large pinch of salt. Reduce the heat, cover, and simmer for about 25 minutes, stirring once or twice, until the vegetables are soft.

3 Allow the soup to cool slightly, then transfer to a food processor or blender and process until smooth.

4 Return the soup to the pan and add the shrimp. Simmer gently for about 10 minutes to reheat.

5 Stir in the tomatoes and dill and remove and discard the bay leaf. Thin the soup with a little more tomato juice, if desired. Remove from the heat and ladle into warmed bowls. Garnish with dill and serve immediately.

shrimp laksa

20–24 large raw unshelled shrimp

2 cups fish stock

pinch of salt

1 tsp peanut oil

2 cups coconut milk

2 tsp Thai fish sauce

½ tbsp lime juice

4 oz/115 g dried medium rice noodles

scant ½ cup bean sprouts

sprigs of fresh cilantro and crispy noodles (optional), to garnish

laksa paste

6 fresh cilantro stalks with leaves

3 large garlic cloves, crushed

1 fresh red chile, seeded and chopped

1 lemongrass stalk, center part only, chopped

1-inch/2.5-cm piece fresh ginger, peeled and chopped

1½ tbsp shrimp paste

½ tsp ground turmeric

2 tbsp peanut oil

1 Peel and devein the shrimp. Put the fish stock, salt, and the shrimp heads, peels, and tails in a saucepan over high heat and slowly bring to a boil. Lower the heat and let simmer for 10 minutes.

2 Meanwhile, make the laksa paste. Put all the ingredients except the oil in a food processor or blender and process. With the motor running, slowly add up to 2 tablespoons of oil just until a paste forms.

3 Heat the oil in a large saucepan over high heat. Add the paste and stir-fry until it is fragrant. Strain the stock through a cheesecloth-lined sieve. Stir the stock into the laksa paste, along with the coconut milk, Thai fish sauce, and lime juice. Bring to a boil, then lower the heat, cover, and let simmer for 30 minutes.

4 Meanwhile, cook the noodles according to the package directions. Drain and set aside. Add the shrimp and bean sprouts to the stew and continue simmering just until the shrimp turn opaque and curl. Divide the noodles between warmed bowls and ladle the stew over. Garnish with the cilantro and crispy noodles and serve immediately.

thai shrimp & scallop soup

SERVES 4

4 cups fish stock

juice of ½ lime

2 tbsp rice wine or sherry

1 leek, sliced

2 shallots, finely chopped

1 tbsp grated fresh ginger

1 fresh red chili, seeded and finely chopped

8 oz/225 g raw shrimp, shelled and deveined

8 oz/225 g scallops, shucked and cleaned

1½ tbsp chopped fresh flat-leaf parsley, plus extra to garnish

salt and pepper

1 Put the stock, lime juice, rice wine, leek, shallots, ginger, and chili in a large saucepan. Bring to a boil over high heat, then reduce the heat, cover, and let simmer for 10 minutes.

2 Add the shrimp, scallops, and parsley, season to taste with salt and pepper, and cook for 1–2 minutes.

3 Remove the pan from the heat and ladle the soup into warmed bowls. Garnish with chopped parsley and serve immediately.

Step 1

Step 1

Step 2

crab & vegetable soup

SERVES 4

2 tbsp chili oil

1 garlic clove, chopped

4 scallions, sliced

2 red bell peppers, seeded and chopped

1 tbsp grated fresh ginger

4 cups fish stock

scant ½ cup coconut milk

scant ½ cup rice wine or sherry

2 tbsp lime juice

1 tbsp grated lime zest

6 kaffir lime leaves, finely shredded

10½ oz/300 g freshly cooked crabmeat

7 oz/200 g freshly cooked crab claws

5½ oz/150 g canned corn kernels, drained

1 tbsp chopped cilantro, plus a few sprigs to garnish

salt and pepper

1 Heat the oil in a large saucepan over medium heat. Add the garlic and scallions and cook, stirring, for about 3 minutes, until slightly softened. Add the bell peppers and ginger and cook for another 4 minutes, stirring. Pour in the stock and season to taste with salt and pepper. Bring to a boil, then lower the heat. Pour in the coconut milk, rice wine, and lime juice and stir in the grated lime zest and kaffir lime leaves. Simmer for 15 minutes.

2 Add the crabmeat and crab claws to the soup with the corn and cilantro. Cook the soup for 15 minutes, until the fish is tender and cooked all the way through.

3 Remove from the heat and ladle into warmed bowls. Garnish with fresh cilantro and serve immediately.

lobster bisque

SERVES 4

1 lb/450 g cooked lobster

3 tbsp butter

1 small carrot, grated

1 celery stalk, finely chopped

1 leek, finely chopped

1 small onion, finely chopped

2 shallots, finely chopped

3 tbsp brandy or Cognac

¼ cup dry white wine

5 cups water

1 tbsp tomato paste

½ cup heavy cream, or to taste

6 tbsp all-purpose flour

2–3 tbsp cold water

salt and pepper

chopped fresh chives, to garnish

1 Pull off the lobster tail. With the legs up, cut the body in half lengthwise. Scoop out the tomalley (the soft pale greenish-gray part) and, if it is a female, the roe (the solid red-orange part). Reserve these together, covered and refrigerated. Remove the meat and cut into bite-sized pieces; cover and refrigerate. Chop the shell into large pieces.

2 Melt half the butter in a large saucepan over medium heat and add the lobster shell pieces. Cook until brown bits begin to stick on the bottom of the pan. Add the carrot, celery, leek, onion, and shallots. Cook, stirring, for 1½–2 minutes. Do not allow to burn. Add the brandy and wine and simmer for 1 minute. Pour the water over, add the tomato paste and a large pinch of salt, and bring to a boil. Reduce the heat, simmer for 30 minutes, and strain the stock through a cheesecloth-lined strainer, discarding the solids.

3 Melt the remaining butter in a small saucepan and add the tomalley and roe, if any. Add the cream, whisk to mix well, remove from the heat, and set aside. Put the flour in a small mixing bowl and very slowly whisk in the water. Stir in a little of the hot stock mixture to make a smooth liquid.

4 Bring the remaining lobster stock to a boil and whisk in the flour mixture. Boil gently for 4–5 minutes, or until the soup thickens. Press the tomalley, roe, and cream mixture through a strainer into the soup. Reheat gently. Remove from the heat and ladle into warmed bowls. Garnish with chives and serve immediately.

fish soup with cider

SERVES 4

2 tsp butter

1 large leek, thinly sliced

2 shallots, finely chopped

½ cup hard cider

1¼ cups fish stock

9 oz/250 g potatoes, diced

1 bay leaf

4 tbsp all-purpose flour

¾ cup milk

¾ cup heavy cream

2 oz/55 g fresh sorrel leaves

12 oz/350 g skinless monkfish or cod fillet, cut into 1-inch/2.5-cm pieces

salt

1 Melt the butter in a large saucepan over medium–low heat. Add the leek and shallots and cook for about 5 minutes, stirring frequently, until they start to soften. Add the cider and bring to a boil.

2 Stir in the stock, potatoes, and bay leaf with a large pinch of salt (unless stock is salty) and bring back to a boil. Reduce the heat, cover, and cook gently for 10 minutes.

3 Put the flour in a small bowl and very slowly whisk in a few tablespoons of the milk to make a thick paste. Stir in a little more to make a smooth liquid.

4 Adjust the heat so the soup simmers gently. Stir in the flour mixture and cook, stirring frequently, for 5 minutes. Add the remaining milk and half the cream. Continue cooking for about 10 minutes, or until the potatoes are tender.

5 Chop the sorrel finely and combine with the remaining cream.

6 Stir the sorrel cream into the soup and add the fish. Continue cooking, stirring occasionally, for about 3 minutes, until the monkfish stiffens or the cod just begins to flake. Remove from the heat and remove and discard the bay leaf. Ladle into warmed bowls and serve immediately.

caribbean fish chowder

SERVES 4

3 tbsp vegetable oil

1 tsp cumin seeds, crushed

1 tsp dried thyme or oregano

1 onion, diced

½ green bell pepper, seeded and diced

1 sweet potato, diced

2–3 fresh green chiles, seeded and very finely chopped

1 garlic clove, very finely chopped

4 cups chicken stock

14 oz/400 g red snapper fillets, skinned and cut into chunks

¼ cup frozen peas

¼ cup frozen corn kernels

½ cup light cream

salt and pepper

3 tbsp chopped fresh cilantro, to garnish

1 Heat the oil with the cumin seeds and thyme in a large saucepan over medium heat. Add the onion, bell pepper, sweet potato, chiles, and garlic and cook, stirring constantly, for 1 minute.

2 Reduce the heat to medium–low, cover, and cook for 10 minutes, or until beginning to soften.

3 Pour in the stock and season generously with salt and pepper. Bring to a boil, then reduce the heat to medium–low, cover, and let simmer for 20 minutes. Meanwhile, prepare the snapper.

4 Add the snapper, peas, corn kernels, and cream. Cook over low heat, uncovered and without boiling, for 7–10 minutes until the fish is just cooked. Remove from the heat and ladle into warmed bowls. Garnish with the chopped cilantro and serve immediately.

Step 1

Step 3

Step 3

whitefish & shrimp chowder

SERVES 4

1 tbsp butter

1 onion, chopped

3 tbsp all-purpose flour

generous 2 cups fish stock

1 bay leaf

generous 2 cups milk

2 tbsp dry white wine

juice and grated rind of 1 lemon

1 lb/450 g whitefish fillets, skinned

4½ oz/125 g frozen corn kernels, thawed

9 oz/250 g shrimp, cooked and peeled

generous ¾ cup heavy cream

salt and pepper

whole cooked shrimp, to garnish

fresh green salad, to serve

1 Melt the butter in a large saucepan over medium heat. Add the onion and cook, stirring, for about 3 minutes, until slightly softened. In a bowl, mix the flour with enough stock to make a smooth paste and stir it into the pan. Cook, stirring, for 2 minutes, then gradually stir in the remaining stock. Add the bay leaf and season to taste with salt and pepper. Bring to a boil, then lower the heat. Pour in the milk and wine, and stir in the lemon juice and grated rind. Simmer for 15 minutes.

2 Rinse the fish under cold running water, then drain, and cut into bite-size chunks. Add them to the soup with the corn. Cook for 15 minutes, until the fish is tender and cooked through. Stir in the shrimp and the cream. Cook for another 2–3 minutes, then remove from the heat and remove and discard the bay leaf.

3 Ladle into warmed bowls, garnish with whole cooked shrimp, and serve immediately with a fresh green salad.

salmon & leek soup

SERVES 4

1 tbsp olive oil

1 large onion, finely chopped

3 large leeks, including green parts, thinly sliced

1 potato, finely diced

2 cups fish stock

3 cups water

1 bay leaf

10½ oz/300 g skinless salmon fillet, cut into ½-inch/1-cm cubes

⅓ cup heavy cream

fresh lemon juice (optional)

salt and pepper

sprigs of fresh chervil or parsley, to garnish

1 Heat the oil in a heavy saucepan over medium heat. Add the onion and leeks and cook for about 3 minutes until they begin to soften.

2 Add the potato, stock, water, and bay leaf with a large pinch of salt. Bring to a boil, reduce the heat, cover, and cook gently for about 25 minutes until the vegetables are tender. Remove and discard the bay leaf.

3 Allow the soup to cool slightly, then transfer about half of it to a food processor or blender and process until smooth. (If using a food processor, strain off the cooking liquid and reserve. Puree half the soup solids with enough cooking liquid to moisten them, then combine with the remaining liquid.)

4 Return the pureed soup to the pan and stir to blend. Reheat gently over medium–low heat.

5 Season the salmon to taste with salt and pepper and add to the soup. Continue cooking for about 5 minutes, stirring occasionally, until the fish is tender and starts to break up. Stir in the cream, taste, and adjust the seasoning, adding a little lemon juice if desired. Remove from the heat and ladle into warmed bowls. Garnish with chervil and serve immediately.

seafood chowder

SERVES 4

2 lb 4 oz/1 kg mussels

4 tbsp all-purpose flour

6¼ cups fish stock

1 tbsp butter

1 large onion, finely chopped

12 oz/350 g skinless whitefish fillets, such as cod or sole

7 oz/200 g cooked or raw shrimp, peeled and deveined

1¼ cups heavy cream

salt and pepper

snipped fresh dill, to garnish

1 Soak the mussels in lightly salted water for 10 minutes. Scrub the shells under cold running water and pull off any beards. Discard any mussels with broken shells or any that refuse to close when tapped. Put the rest in a large heavy saucepan with a little water, bring to the boil, and cook over high heat for 4 minutes, or until the mussels open. Remove from the heat and discard any that remain closed. When they are cool enough to handle, remove the mussels from the shells, adding any additional juices to the cooking liquid. Strain the cooking liquid through a cheesecloth-lined strainer and reserve.

2 Put the flour in a mixing bowl and very slowly whisk in enough of the stock to make a thick paste. Whisk in a little more stock to make a smooth liquid. Melt the butter in a heavy saucepan over medium–low heat. Add the onion, cover, and cook for about 5 minutes, stirring frequently, until it softens.

3 Add the remaining fish stock and bring to a boil. Slowly whisk in the flour mixture until well combined and bring back to a boil, whisking constantly. Add the mussel cooking liquid and season to taste with salt and pepper. Reduce the heat and simmer, partially covered, for 15 minutes.

4 Add the fish and mussels and continue simmering, stirring occasionally, for about 5 minutes, or until the fish is cooked and begins to flake. Stir in the shrimp and cream. Reheat gently. Remove from the heat and ladle into warmed bowls. Garnish with dill and serve immediately.

cold cucumber & smoked salmon soup

SERVES 4

2 tsp oil

1 large onion, finely chopped

1 large cucumber, peeled, seeded, and sliced

1 small potato, diced

1 celery stalk, finely chopped

4 cups chicken or vegetable stock

1⅔ cups heavy cream

5½ oz/150 g smoked salmon, finely diced

2 tbsp chopped fresh chives

salt and pepper

1 Heat the oil in a large saucepan over medium heat. Add the onion and cook for about 3 minutes, until it begins to soften.

2 Add the cucumber, potato, celery, and stock, along with a large pinch of salt, if using unsalted stock. Bring to a boil, reduce the heat, cover, and cook gently for about 20 minutes or until the vegetables are tender.

3 Allow the soup to cool slightly, then transfer to a food processor or blender and process until smooth. Puree the soup until smooth. (If using a food processor, strain off the cooking liquid and reserve it. Puree the soup solids with enough cooking liquid to moisten them, then combine with the remaining liquid.)

4 Transfer the soup to a large bowl. Cover and refrigerate until cold.

5 Stir the cream, salmon, and chives into the soup. If time permits, chill for at least 1 hour to allow the flavors to blend. Season to taste with salt and pepper. Ladle into chilled bowls and serve immediately.

VARIATION

For a more distinctive flavor, add 1 tablespoon of chopped fresh dill to the saucepan along with the cucumber, potato, celery, and stock. Cook as above; ladle into chilled bowls, garnish with dill sprigs and serve immediately.

Meat
Feast

chunky potato & beef soup

SERVES 4

2 tbsp vegetable oil

8 oz/225 g lean braising steak, cut into strips

8 oz/225 g new potatoes, halved

1 carrot, diced

2 celery stalks, sliced

2 leeks, sliced

3½ cups beef stock

8 baby corn, sliced

1 bouquet garni

2 tbsp dry sherry

salt and pepper

chopped fresh parsley, to garnish

1 Heat the vegetable oil in a large saucepan. Add the strips of meat to the pan and cook for 3 minutes, turning constantly. Add the potatoes, carrot, celery, and leeks to the pan. Cook for an additional 5 minutes, stirring.

2 Pour the beef stock into the pan and bring to a boil. Reduce the heat until the liquid is simmering, then add the baby corn and the bouquet garni. Cook for an additional 20 minutes, or until cooked through.

3 Remove from the heat and remove and discard the bouquet garni. Stir the dry sherry into the soup. Season to taste with salt and pepper.

4 Ladle the soup into warmed bowls, garnish with chopped parsley, and serve immediately.

beef & vegetable soup

SERVES 4

⅓ cup pearl barley, rinsed and drained

5 cups beef stock

1 tsp dried mixed herbs

8 oz/225 g lean sirloin or porterhouse steak

1 large carrot, diced

1 leek, shredded

1 medium onion, chopped

2 celery stalks, sliced

salt and pepper

2 tbsp chopped fresh parsley, to garnish

1 Place the pearl barley in a large saucepan. Pour the stock over it and add the mixed herbs. Bring to a boil, cover, and simmer gently over low heat for 10 minutes. Meanwhile, trim any fat from the beef and cut the meat into thin strips.

2 Skim away any foam that has risen to the surface. Add the beef, carrot, leek, onion, and celery to the pan. Bring back to a boil, cover, and simmer for about 1 hour, or until the pearl barley, beef, and vegetables are just tender.

3 Remove from the heat. Skim away any remaining foam that has risen to the surface. Blot the surface with absorbent paper towels to remove any fat.

4 Ladle the soup into warmed bowls, garnish with chopped parsley, and serve immediately.

beef & bean soup

SERVES 6

2 tbsp vegetable oil

1 large onion, finely chopped

2 garlic cloves, finely chopped

1 green bell pepper, seeded and sliced

2 carrots, sliced

14 oz/400 g canned black-eyed peas

1 cup fresh ground beef

1 tsp each ground cumin, chili powder, and paprika

¼ head of cabbage, sliced

8 oz/225 g tomatoes, peeled and chopped

2½ cups beef stock

salt and pepper

1 Heat the oil in a large saucepan over medium heat. Add the onion and garlic and cook, stirring frequently, for 5 minutes, or until softened. Add the bell pepper and carrots and cook for an additional 5 minutes.

2 Meanwhile, drain the peas, reserving the liquid from the can. Place two thirds of the peas, reserving the remainder, in a food processor or blender with the pea liquid and process until smooth.

3 Add the ground beef to the pan and cook, stirring constantly to break up any lumps, until well browned. Add the spices and cook, stirring, for 2 minutes. Add the cabbage, tomatoes, stock, and pureed peas and season to taste with salt and pepper. Bring to a boil, then reduce the heat, cover, and let simmer for 15 minutes, or until the vegetables are tender.

4 Stir in the reserved peas, cover, and simmer for an additional 5 minutes. Remove from the heat and ladle into warmed bowls. Serve immediately.

ground beef and cilantro soup

SERVES 4–6

2 cups ground beef

6¼ cups chicken stock

3 egg whites, lightly beaten

1 tsp salt

½ tsp white pepper

1 tbsp finely chopped fresh ginger

1 tbsp finely chopped scallions

4–5 tbsp finely chopped cilantro, tough stems discarded

marinade

1 tsp salt

1 tsp sugar

1 tsp Chinese rice wine

1 tsp light soy sauce

1 Combine all the ingredients for the marinade in a bowl and marinate the beef for 20 minutes.

2 Bring the stock to a boil in a saucepan. Add the beef, stirring to break up any clumps, and simmer for 10 minutes.

3 Slowly add the egg whites, stirring rapidly so that they form into fine shreds. Add the salt and pepper and taste to check the seasoning.

4 Place the ginger, scallions and cilantro into the warmed bowls, and ladle the soup on top. Serve immediately.

Step 1

Step 2

Step 3

mexican-style beef & rice soup

SERVES 4

3 tbsp olive oil

1 lb 2 oz/500 g boneless braising beef, cut into 1-inch/2.5-cm pieces

⅔ cup red wine

1 onion, finely chopped

1 green bell pepper, seeded and finely chopped

1 small fresh red chile, seeded and finely chopped

2 garlic cloves, finely chopped

1 carrot, finely chopped

¼ tsp coriander

¼ tsp ground cumin

pinch of ground cumin

¼ tsp dried oregano

1 bay leaf

grated rind of ½ orange

14 oz/400 g canned chopped tomatoes

5 cups beef stock

¼ cup long-grain white rice

3 tbsp raisins

½ oz/15 g semisweet chocolate, melted

1 Heat half the oil in a large skillet over medium–high heat. Add the meat in one layer and cook until well browned, turning to color all sides. Remove the pan from the heat and pour in the wine.

2 Heat the remaining oil in a large saucepan over medium heat. Add the onion, cover, and cook for about 3 minutes, stirring occasionally, until just softened. Add the green bell pepper, chile, garlic, and carrot and continue cooking, covered, for 3 minutes.

3 Add the coriander, cumin, cinnamon, oregano, bay leaf, and orange rind. Stir in the tomatoes and stock, along with the beef and wine mixture. Bring almost to a boil and when the mixture begins to bubble, reduce the heat to low. Cover and simmer gently, stirring occasionally, for about 1 hour until the meat is tender.

4 Stir in the rice, raisins, and chocolate, and continue cooking, stirring occasionally, for about 30 minutes until the rice is tender. Remove from the heat and remove and discard the bay leaf. Ladle into warmed bowls and serve immediately.

spicy beef & noodle soup

SERVES 4

4 cups beef stock

⅔ cup vegetable or peanut oil

3 oz/85 g rice vermicelli noodles

2 shallots, thinly sliced

2 garlic cloves, crushed

1-inch/2.5-cm piece fresh ginger, thinly sliced

8 oz/225 g piece beef tenderloin, cut into thin strips

2 tbsp Thai green curry paste

2 tbsp soy sauce

1 tbsp Thai fish sauce

fresh cilantro leaves, to garnish

1 Pour the stock into a large saucepan and bring to a boil. Meanwhile, heat the oil in a wok or large skillet. Add a third of the noodles and cook for 10–20 seconds, until they have puffed up. Lift out with tongs, drain on paper towels, and set aside. Discard all but 2 tablespoons of the oil.

2 Add the shallots, garlic, and ginger to the wok or skillet and stir-fry for 1 minute. Add the beef and curry paste and stir-fry for an additional 3–4 minutes, until tender.

3 Add the beef mixture, the uncooked noodles, soy sauce, and fish sauce to the pan of stock and simmer for 2–3 minutes, until the noodles have swelled. Remove from the heat and ladle into warmed bowls. Garnish with cilantro leaves and serve immediately with the reserved noodles.

beef broth with herbs & vegetables

SERVES 4–6

7 oz/200 g celeriac, peeled and finely diced

2 large carrots, finely diced

2 tsp chopped fresh marjoram leaves

2 tsp chopped fresh parsley

2 plum tomatoes, skinned, seeded, and diced

salt and pepper

beef stock

1 lb 4 oz/550g boneless beef shin or braising beef, cut into large cubes

1 lb 10 oz/750 g veal, beef, or pork bones

2 onions, quartered

10 cups water

4 garlic cloves, sliced

2 carrots, sliced

1 large leek, sliced

1 celery stalk, cut into 2-inch/5-cm pieces

1 bay leaf

4–5 sprigs of fresh thyme, or ¼ tsp dried thyme

salt

1 Preheat the oven to 375°F/190°C. To make the stock, trim as much fat as possible from the beef and put in a large roasting pan with the bones and onions. Roast for 30–40 minutes, turning once or twice. Transfer to a large flameproof casserole and discard the fat.

2 Add the water and bring to a boil, skimming off any foam that rises to the surface. Reduce the heat and add the garlic, carrots, leek, celery, bay leaf, thyme, and salt. Simmer very gently, uncovered, for 4 hours. Do not stir. If the ingredients emerge from the liquid, top up with water.

3 Gently ladle the stock through a cheesecloth-lined strainer into a large container and remove as much fat as possible. Save the meat for another purpose, if desired, and remove and discard the bones and vegetables. (There should be about 8 cups of stock.)

4 Boil the stock very gently until it is reduced to 6¼ cups, or if the stock already has concentrated flavor, measure out that amount and save the rest for another purpose.

5 Bring a saucepan of salted water to a boil and drop in the celeriac and carrots. Reduce the heat, cover, and boil gently for about 15 minutes until tender. Drain and remove and discard the bay leaf.

6 Add the marjoram and parsley to the boiling beef stock. Remove from the heat. Divide the cooked vegetables and diced tomatoes between warmed bowls. Ladle over the boiling stock and serve immediately.

japanese-style beef soup

SERVES 2

4 oz/115 g dried udon or soba noodles

2 tbsp brown rice miso

2½ cups vegetable stock

1 tbsp mirin or rice wine

¾ cup baby corn, halved diagonally

1¼ cups white mushrooms, halved

1½ cups bean sprouts

1½ oz/40 g baby spinach leaves

1 tbsp peanut or sunflower oil

10 oz/280 g thin cut porterhouse or sirloin steak, cut into bite-size pieces

1 small fresh red chile, very thinly sliced

1 Cook the noodles according to the package directions. Drain and set aside.

2 Blend the miso with a little of the stock. Heat the remaining stock in a saucepan. Add the mirin, corn, and mushrooms and simmer for 3 minutes. Add the bean sprouts and simmer for an additional minute. Remove from the heat and stir in the miso. Add the spinach and cover the pan.

3 Heat a wok or large skillet over high heat. Add the oil and stir-fry the steak with the chile for 1–2 minutes, until browned, or cooked to your taste. Remove from the heat.

4 Pour boiling water over the noodles to reheat them. Drain well, then divide between warmed bowls. Ladle the miso-flavored soup and vegetables over the noodles. Top with the stir-fried beef and serve immediately.

Step 1

Step 2

Step 3

beef consommé with eggs & parmesan

SERVES 4

6⅓ cups beef consommé or beef stock

3 eggs

½ cup fresh white breadcrumbs

½ cup Parmesan cheese, freshly grated

salt

1 Pour the consommé or stock into a saucepan and heat gently, stirring occasionally.

2 Meanwhile, beat the eggs in a bowl until combined, then stir in the breadcrumbs and Parmesan cheese. Season to taste with salt.

3 As soon as the consommé or stock comes to a boil, add the egg mixture. When it floats to the surface, stir with a fork to break it up. Remove from the heat and ladle into warmed bowls. Serve immediately.

hearty winter soup

SERVES 4

1 tbsp vegetable oil

1 lb 2 oz/500 g lean neck of lamb

1 large onion, sliced

2 carrots, sliced

2 leeks, sliced

4 cups vegetable stock

1 bay leaf

fresh parsley sprigs

2 oz/55 g pearl barley, rinsed and drained

salt and pepper

1 Heat the vegetable oil in a large, heavy saucepan and add the lamb, turning to seal and brown on both sides. Lift the lamb out of the pan and set aside until ready to use.

2 Add the onion, carrots, and leeks to the pan and cook gently for about 3 minutes.

3 Return the lamb to the pan and add the vegetable stock, bay leaf, parsley, and pearl barley to the pan. Bring the mixture to a boil, then reduce the heat. Cover and simmer for 1½–2 hours.

4 Remove and discard the bay leaf. Lift the pieces of lamb from the broth and allow them to cool slightly. Remove the bones and any fat and chop the meat. Return the lamb to the broth and reheat gently. Season to taste with salt and pepper.

5 It is advisable to prepare this soup a day ahead, then leave it to cool, cover, and refrigerate overnight. When ready to serve, remove and discard the layer of fat from the surface and reheat the soup gently. Remove from the heat and ladle into warmed bowls. Serve immediately.

asian lamb soup

SERVES 4

5½ oz/150 g lean tender lamb, such as neck fillet or leg steak

2 garlic cloves, very finely chopped

2 tbsp soy sauce

5 cups chicken stock

1 tbsp grated fresh ginger

2-inch/5-cm piece lemongrass, sliced into very thin rounds

¼ tsp chili paste, or to taste

6–8 cherry tomatoes, quartered

4 scallions, thinly sliced

1¾ oz/50 g bean sprouts, snapped in half

2 tbsp cilantro leaves

1 tsp olive oil

1 Trim all visible fat from the lamb and slice the meat thinly. Cut the slices into bite-sized pieces. Spread the meat in one layer on a plate and sprinkle the garlic and 1 tablespoon of the soy sauce over the top. Leave to marinate, covered, for at least 10 minutes or up to 1 hour.

2 Put the stock in a saucepan with the ginger, lemongrass, remaining soy sauce, and the chili paste. Bring just to a boil, reduce the heat, cover, and simmer for 10–15 minutes.

3 When ready to serve the soup, drop the tomatoes, scallions, bean sprouts, and cilantro leaves into the stock.

4 Heat the oil in a skillet and add the lamb with its marinade. Stir-fry the lamb just until it is no longer red and divide among warmed bowls. Ladle over the hot stock and serve immediately.

lamb & rice soup

SERVES 4

5½ oz/150 g lean lamb

scant ¼ cup rice

3½ cups lamb stock

1 leek, sliced

1 garlic clove, thinly sliced

2 tsp light soy sauce

1 tsp rice wine vinegar

1 medium open-cap mushroom, thinly sliced

salt

1 Trim any visible fat from the lamb and cut the meat into thin strips. Set aside until required.

2 Bring a large saucepan of lightly salted water to a boil and add the rice. Return to a boil, stir once, reduce the heat, and cook for 10–15 minutes, or until tender. Drain the cooked rice, rinse under cold running water, drain again, and set aside.

3 Place the lamb stock in a large pan and bring to a boil. Add the lamb strips, leek, garlic, soy sauce, and rice wine vinegar, reduce the heat, cover, and let simmer for 10 minutes, or until the lamb is tender and cooked through.

4 Add the mushroom slices and cooked rice to the pan and cook for an additional 2–3 minutes, or until the mushrooms are completely cooked through. Remove from the heat and ladle into warmed bowls. Serve immediately.

Step 1

Step 3

Step 4

lamb & harissa soup

SERVES 4

2 eggplants

3 tbsp olive oil

6 lamb shanks

1 small onion, chopped

1¾ cups chicken stock

8 cups water

14 oz/400 g sweet potatoes, cut into chunks

2-inch/5-cm piece cinnamon stick

1 tsp ground cumin

2 tbsp chopped fresh cilantro

harissa

2 red bell peppers, roasted, peeled, seeded, and chopped

½ tsp coriander seeds, dry-roasted

1 oz/25 g fresh red chiles, chopped

2 garlic cloves, chopped

2 tsp caraway seeds

olive oil

salt

1 Preheat the oven to 400°F/200°C. Prick the eggplants, place on a baking sheet, and bake for 1 hour. When cool, peel and chop.

2 Heat the oil in a saucepan. Add the lamb and cook until browned. Add the onion, stock, and water. Bring to a boil. Reduce the heat and let simmer for 1 hour.

3 For the harissa, place the bell peppers, coriander seeds, chiles, garlic, and caraway seeds in a food processor or blender and process. With the motor running, add enough oil to make a paste. Season to taste with salt, then spoon into a jar. Cover with oil, seal, and chill.

4 Remove the shanks from the stock, cut off the meat, and chop. Add the sweet potatoes, cinnamon, and cumin to the stock, bring to a boil, cover, and simmer for 20 minutes. Remove and discard the cinnamon and process the mixture in a food processor or blender with the eggplant. Return to the pan, add the lamb and cilantro, and reheat gently. Remove from the heat and ladle into warmed bowls. Serve immediately with the harissa.

spicy lamb soup with chickpeas

SERVES 4–6

1–2 tbsp olive oil

1 lb/450 g lean boneless lamb, trimmed of fat and cut into ½-inch/1-cm cubes

1 onion, finely chopped

2–3 garlic cloves, crushed

5 cups water

14 oz/400 g canned chopped tomatoes

1 bay leaf

½ tsp each of dried thyme and oregano

pinch of ground cinnamon

½ tsp each of ground cumin and turmeric

1 tsp harissa (see page 134)

14 oz/400 g canned chickpeas, rinsed and drained

1 each of carrot, potato, and zucchini, diced

3½ oz/100 g fresh peas

fresh mint sprigs, to garnish

1. Heat 1 tablespoon of the oil in a large saucepan or cast-iron casserole over medium–high heat. Add the lamb, in batches if necessary to avoid crowding the pan, and cook until evenly browned on all sides, adding a little more oil if needed. Remove the meat with a slotted spoon.

2. Reduce the heat and add the onion and garlic to the pan. Cook, stirring frequently, for 1–2 minutes.

3. Add the water and return all the meat to the pan. Bring just to a boil, skimming off any foam that rises to the surface. Reduce the heat and stir in the tomatoes, bay leaf, thyme, oregano, cinnamon, cumin, turmeric, and harissa. Simmer for about 1 hour, or until the meat is very tender. Remove and discard the bay leaf.

4. Stir in the chickpeas, carrot, and potato and simmer for 15 minutes. Add the zucchini and peas and continue simmering for 15–20 minutes, or until all the vegetables are tender.

5. Remove from the heat and ladle into warmed bowls. Garnish with mint and serve immediately.

bacon & lentil soup

SERVES 6

1 lb/450 g thick, smoked bacon strips, diced

1 onion, chopped

2 carrots, sliced

2 celery stalks, chopped

1 turnip, chopped

1 large potato, chopped

generous 2¼ cups fresh green lentils

1 bouquet garni

4 cups water or chicken stock

salt and pepper

1 Heat a large, heavy saucepan or flameproof casserole. Add the bacon and cook over medium heat, stirring, for 4–5 minutes, or until the fat runs. Add the chopped onion, carrots, celery, turnip, and potato and cook, stirring frequently, for 5 minutes.

2 Add the lentils and bouquet garni and pour in the water. Bring to a boil, reduce the heat, and simmer for 1 hour, or until the lentils are tender.

3 Remove from the heat and remove and discard the bouquet garni. Season the soup to taste with pepper, and with salt if necessary. Ladle into warmed bowls and serve immediately.

cheese & bacon soup

SERVES 4

2 tbsp butter

2 garlic cloves, chopped

1 large onion, sliced

9 oz/250 g smoked bacon, chopped

2 large leeks, sliced

2 tbsp all-purpose flour

4 cups vegetable stock

1 lb/450 g potatoes, chopped

scant ½ cup heavy cream

3 cups grated cheddar cheese, plus extra to garnish

salt and pepper

1 Melt the butter in a large saucepan over medium heat. Add the garlic and onion and cook, stirring, for 3 minutes, until slightly softened. Add the chopped bacon and leeks and cook for another 3 minutes, stirring.

2 In a bowl, mix the flour with enough stock to make a smooth paste and stir it into the pan. Cook, stirring, for 2 minutes. Pour in the remaining stock, then add the potatoes. Season to taste with salt and pepper. Bring the soup to a boil, then lower the heat and simmer gently for 25 minutes, until the potatoes are tender and cooked through.

3 Stir in the cream and cook for 5 minutes, then gradually stir in the cheese until melted. Remove from the heat and ladle into warmed bowls. Garnish with grated cheddar cheese and serve immediately.

Step 1

Step 2

Step 2

split pea & ham soup

SERVES 6–8

1 lb 2 oz/500 g split green peas

1 tbsp olive oil

1 large onion, finely chopped

1 large carrot, finely chopped

1 celery stalk, finely chopped

4 cups chicken or vegetable stock

4 cups water

8 oz/225 g lean smoked ham, finely diced

¼ tsp dried thyme

¼ tsp dried marjoram

1 bay leaf

salt and pepper

1 Rinse the peas under cold running water. Put in a saucepan and cover generously with water. Bring to a boil and boil for 3 minutes, skimming off the foam from the surface. Drain and set aside.

2 Heat the oil in a large saucepan over medium heat. Add the onion and cook for 3–4 minutes, stirring occasionally, until just softened.

3 Add the carrot and celery and continue cooking for 2 minutes. Add the peas, pour over the stock and water, and stir to combine.

4 Bring just to a boil and stir the ham into the soup. Add the thyme, marjoram, and bay leaf. Reduce the heat, cover, and cook gently for 1–1½ hours, or until the ingredients are very soft. Remove from the heat and remove and discard the bay leaf.

5 Season to taste with salt and pepper. Ladle into warmed soup bowls and serve immediately.

pork & vegetable broth

SERVES 4

1 tbsp chili oil

1 garlic clove, chopped

3 scallions, sliced

1 red bell pepper, seeded and finely sliced

2 tbsp cornstarch

4 cups vegetable stock

1 tbsp soy sauce

2 tbsp rice wine or dry sherry

5½ oz/150 g pork tenderloin, sliced

1 tbsp finely chopped lemongrass

1 small red chile, seeded and finely chopped

1 tbsp grated fresh ginger

4 oz/115 g fine egg noodles

7 oz/200 g canned water chestnuts, drained and sliced

salt and pepper

1 Heat the oil in a large saucepan. Add the garlic and scallions and cook over medium heat, stirring, for 3 minutes, until slightly softened. Add the bell pepper and cook for an additional 5 minutes, stirring.

2 In a bowl, mix the cornstarch with enough of the stock to make a smooth paste and stir it into the pan. Cook, stirring, for 2 minutes. Stir in the remaining stock, the soy sauce, and the rice wine, then add the pork, lemongrass, chile, and ginger. Season to taste with salt and pepper. Bring to a boil, then lower the heat and simmer for 25 minutes.

3 Bring a separate saucepan of water to a boil, add the noodles, and cook for 3 minutes, or according to the package directions. Remove from the heat, drain, then add the noodles to the soup along with the water chestnuts. Remove from the heat and ladle into warmed bowls. Serve immediately.

wonton soup

SERVES 6–8

8 cups chicken soup

2 tsp salt

½ tsp white pepper

2 tbsp finely chopped scallions

1 tbsp chopped fresh cilantro leaves, to garnish

wontons

6 oz/175 g ground pork, not too lean

8 oz/225 g raw shrimp, peeled, deveined, and chopped

½ tsp finely chopped fresh ginger

1 tbsp light soy sauce

1 tbsp Chinese rice wine

2 tsp finely chopped scallions

pinch of sugar

pinch of white pepper

dash of sesame oil

30 square wonton wrappers

1 egg white, lightly beaten

1 For the wonton filling, mix together the pork, shrimp, ginger, soy sauce, rice wine, scallions, sugar, pepper, and sesame oil, and stir well until the texture is thick and pasty. Set aside for at least 20 minutes.

2 To make the wontons, place a teaspoon of the filling at the center of a wrapper. Brush the edges with a little egg white. Bring the opposite points toward each other and press the edges together, creating a flowerlike shape. Repeat with the remaining wrappers and filling.

3 To make the soup, bring the stock to a boil and add the salt and the pepper (omit the salt if using a stock that is already salty). Boil the wontons in the stock for about 5 minutes until the wrappers begin to wrinkle around the filling.

4 Divide the scallions between warmed bowls. Spoon in the wontons and ladle the soup over the top. Garnish with the cilantro leaves and serve immediately.

chinese pork & potato broth

SERVES 4

4 cups chicken stock

2 large potatoes, diced

2 tbsp rice wine vinegar

2 tbsp cornstarch

4 tbsp water

4½ oz/125 g pork tenderloin, sliced

1 tbsp light soy sauce

1 tsp sesame oil

1 carrot, cut into very thin strips

1 tsp chopped fresh ginger

3 scallions, thinly sliced

1 red bell pepper, seeded and sliced

8 oz/225 g canned bamboo shoots, drained

1 Place the stock, potatoes, and 1 tablespoon of the vinegar in a saucepan and bring to a boil. Reduce the heat until the stock is just simmering.

2 Mix the cornstarch with the water, then stir into the hot stock.

3 Return the stock to a boil, stirring until thickened, then reduce the heat until it is just simmering again.

4 Place the pork slices in a dish and season with the remaining vinegar, the soy sauce, and the sesame oil.

5 Add the pork slices, carrot strips, and ginger to the stock and cook for 10 minutes. Stir in the scallions, bell pepper, and bamboo shoots. Cook for an additional 5 minutes. Remove from the heat and ladle into warmed bowls. Serve immediately.

Step 1

Step 4

Step 5

pork chili soup

SERVES 4

2 tsp olive oil

1 lb 2 oz/500 g fresh lean ground pork

1 onion, finely chopped

1 celery stalk, finely chopped

1 red bell pepper, seeded, and finely chopped

2–3 garlic cloves, finely chopped

3 tbsp tomato paste

14 oz/400 g canned chopped tomatoes

2 cups chicken or meat stock

a pinch of coriander

a pinch of ground cumin

¼ tsp dried oregano

1 tsp mild chili powder, or to taste

salt and pepper

sour cream, to serve

1 Heat the oil in a large saucepan over medium–high heat. Add the pork, season to taste with salt and pepper, and cook until no longer pink, stirring frequently. Reduce the heat to medium and add the onion, celery, red bell pepper, and garlic. Cover and continue cooking for 5 minutes, stirring occasionally, until the onion has softened.

2 Add the tomato paste, tomatoes, and the stock. Add the coriander, cumin, oregano, and chili powder. Stir to combine well.

3 Bring just to a boil, reduce the heat to low, cover, and simmer for 30–40 minutes, or until all the vegetables are very tender. Taste and adjust the seasoning, adding more chili powder if you like it hotter. Remove from the heat.

4 Ladle the soup into warmed bowls and serve immediately with a spoonful of sour cream.

chorizo & red kidney bean soup

SERVES 4

2 tbsp olive oil

2 garlic cloves, chopped

2 red onions, chopped

1 red bell pepper, seeded and chopped

2 tbsp cornstarch

4 cups vegetable stock

1 lb/450 g potatoes, peeled, halved, and sliced

5½ oz/150 g chorizo, sliced

2 zucchini, sliced

7 oz/200 g canned red kidney beans, drained

½ cup heavy cream

salt and pepper

1 Heat the oil in a large saucepan. Add the garlic and onions and cook over medium heat, stirring, for 3 minutes, or until slightly softened. Add the bell pepper and cook for another 3 minutes, stirring. In a bowl, mix the cornstarch with enough stock to make a smooth paste and stir it into the pan. Cook, stirring, for 2 minutes.

2 Stir in the remaining stock, then add the potatoes and season to taste with salt and pepper. Bring to a boil, then lower the heat and simmer for 25 minutes, until the vegetables are tender.

3 Add the chorizo, zucchini, and kidney beans to the pan. Cook for 10 minutes, then stir in the cream and cook for another 5 minutes. Remove from the heat and ladle into warmed bowls. Serve immediately.

corn, chorizo & smoked chili soup

SERVES 4

1 tbsp corn oil

2 onions, chopped

1 lb 4 oz/550 g frozen corn kernels, thawed

2½ cups chicken stock

2 cups milk

4 chipotle chiles, seeded and finely chopped

2 garlic cloves, finely chopped

2 oz/55 g thinly sliced chorizo sausage

2 tbsp lime juice

2 tbsp chopped fresh cilantro

salt

1 Heat the oil in a large heavy saucepan. Add the onions and cook over low heat, stirring occasionally, for 5 minutes, or until softened. Stir in the corn, cover, and cook for an additional 3 minutes.

2 Add the stock, half the milk, the chiles, and garlic and season to taste with salt. Bring to a boil, reduce the heat, then cover and simmer for 15–20 minutes.

3 Stir in the remaining milk. Set aside about ¾ cup of the soup solids, draining off as much liquid as possible. Transfer the remaining soup to a food processor or blender and process to a coarse puree.

4 Return the soup to the pan and stir in the reserved soup solids, the chorizo, lime juice, and cilantro. Reheat to simmering point, stirring constantly. Remove from the heat and ladle into warmed bowls. Serve immediately.

sausage & red cabbage soup

SERVES 4

2 tbsp olive oil

1 garlic clove, chopped

1 large onion, chopped

1 large leek, sliced

2 tbsp cornstarch

4 cups vegetable stock

1 lb/450 g potatoes, sliced

7 oz/200 g skinless sausages, sliced

5½ oz/150 g red cabbage, chopped

7 oz/200 g canned black-eyed peas, drained

½ cup heavy cream

salt and pepper

ground paprika, to garnish

1 Heat the oil in a large saucepan . Add the garlic and onion and cook over medium heat, stirring, for 3 minutes, until slightly softened. Add the leek and cook for another 3 minutes, stirring.

2 In a bowl, mix the cornstarch with enough stock to make a smooth paste, then stir it into the pan. Cook, stirring, for 2 minutes. Stir in the remaining stock, then add the potatoes and sausages. Season to taste with salt and pepper. Bring to a boil, then lower the heat and simmer for 25 minutes.

3 Add the red cabbage and black-eyed peas and cook for 10 minutes, then stir in the cream and cook for another 5 minutes. Remove from the heat and ladle into warmed bowls. Garnish with ground paprika and serve immediately.

VARIATION

For a spicier version, use 10½ oz/300 g skinless sausages or pork sausage meat. In a bowl, combine beaten sausage meat with 1 tablespoon of ground paprika, ½ teaspoon of ground caraway seeds, and season to taste with salt and pepper. Form into 16 balls, brown on all sides in the oil, remove and set aside. Use 1 tablespoon of cornstarch to thicken the stock, 7 oz/200 g potatoes, cut into ½-inch/1-cm cubes, 7 oz/200 g red cabbage, and 3½ oz/100 ml sour cream instead of the heavy cream. Return the meatballs to the pot with the potatoes.

4

Perfect
Poultry

chicken, mushroom & barley soup

SERVES 4

2¾ oz/75 g pearl barley, rinsed and drained

2 tbsp butter

1 large onion, sliced

1 large leek, sliced

4 cups chicken stock

1 lb/450 g skinless chicken breasts, chopped

9 oz/250 g cremini mushrooms, sliced

1 large carrot, chopped

1 tbsp chopped fresh oregano

1 bay leaf

salt and pepper

fresh flat-leaf parsley sprigs, to garnish

fresh French bread, to serve

1 Bring a saucepan of water to a boil. Add the barley and boil over high heat for 5 minutes, skimming off any foam that rises to the surface. Remove from the heat and set aside.

2 Melt the butter in a large saucepan. Add the onion and cook over medium heat, stirring, for 3 minutes, until slightly softened. Add the leek and cook for another 4 minutes, stirring. Stir in the stock, then drain the barley and add to the pan. Season to taste with salt and pepper. Bring to a boil, then lower the heat and simmer for 45 minutes. Add the chicken, mushrooms, carrot, oregano, and bay leaf. Cook for another 30 minutes.

3 Remove from the heat and remove and discard the bay leaf. Ladle into warmed bowls, garnish with sprigs of fresh flat-leaf parsley, and serve immediately with fresh French bread.

chicken ravioli in tarragon broth

SERVES 6

8 cups chicken stock

2 tbsp finely chopped fresh tarragon leaves

freshly grated Parmesan cheese, to garnish

pasta dough

1 cup all-purpose flour, plus extra if needed

2 tbsp fresh tarragon leaves, stems removed

pinch of salt

1 egg

1 egg, separated

1 tsp extra virgin olive oil

2–3 tbsp water

filling

7 oz/200 g cooked chicken, coarsely chopped

½ tsp grated lemon rind

2 tbsp chopped mixed fresh tarragon, chives, and parsley

4 tbsp heavy cream

salt and pepper

1 To make the pasta, combine the flour, tarragon, and salt in a food processor or blender. Beat together the egg, egg yolk, oil, and 2 tablespoons of water. With the machine running, pour in the egg mixture and process until it forms a ball. Wrap and chill for 30 minutes. Reserve the egg white.

2 To make the filling, put the chicken, lemon rind, and mixed herbs in a food processor and season to taste with salt and pepper. Chop finely by pulsing; do not overprocess. Scrape into a bowl and stir in the cream.

3 Divide the pasta dough in half. Cover one half and roll the other half on a floured surface as thinly as possible. Cut out rectangles about 4 x 2 inches/10 x 5 cm.

4 Place a teaspoon of filling on one half of each rectangle. Brush the edges with egg white and fold in half. Press the edges to seal. Arrange the ravioli on a baking sheet, dusted with flour. Repeat with the remaining dough. Allow the ravioli to dry for about 15 minutes or chill for 1–2 hours.

5 Bring a large saucepan of water to a boil. Drop in half the ravioli and cook for 12–15 minutes, until just tender. Drain well and cook the remainder.

6 Put the stock and tarragon in a large saucepan. Bring to a boil, then cover and simmer for 15 minutes. Add the ravioli and simmer for 5 minutes. Garnish with Parmesan cheese and ladle into warmed bowls. Serve immediately.

chicken, rice & vegetable soup

SERVES 4

6¼ cups chicken stock

2 small carrots, very thinly sliced

1 celery stalk, finely diced

1 baby leek, halved lengthwise and thinly sliced

4 oz/115 g young green peas, defrosted if frozen

1 cup cooked rice

5½ oz/150 g cooked chicken, sliced

2 tsp chopped fresh tarragon

1 tbsp chopped fresh parsley

salt and pepper

fresh parsley sprigs, to garnish

1 Put the stock in a large saucepan and add the carrots, celery, and leek. Bring to a boil, reduce the heat to low, and simmer gently, partially covered, for 10 minutes.

2 Stir in the young green peas, rice, and chicken and continue cooking for an additional 10–15 minutes, or until the vegetables are tender.

3 Add the chopped tarragon and parsley. Remove from the heat and ladle into warmed bowls. Garnish with parsley and serve immediately.

chicken, avocado & chipotle soup

6¼ cups chicken stock

2–3 garlic cloves, finely chopped

1–2 dried chipotle chiles, cut into very thin strips

1 avocado

lime or lemon juice, for tossing

3–5 scallions, thinly sliced

12–14 oz/350–400 g cooked chicken breast meat, torn or cut into shreds or thin strips

2 tbsp chopped fresh cilantro

1 lime, cut into wedges and a handful of tortilla chips (optional), to serve

1 Place the stock in a large, heavy saucepan with the garlic and chiles and bring to a boil.

2 Meanwhile, cut the avocado in half around the pit. Twist apart, then remove the pit with a knife. Carefully peel off the skin, dice the flesh, and toss in lime juice to prevent discoloration.

3 Divide the scallions, chicken, avocado, and cilantro between warmed bowls.

4 Ladle the hot stock over and serve immediately with lime wedges and a handful of tortilla chips, if wished.

Step 1

Step 2

Step 2

cream of chicken soup

SERVES 4

3 tbsp butter

4 shallots, chopped

1 leek, sliced

1 lb/450 g skinless chicken breasts, chopped

2½ cups chicken stock

1 tbsp chopped fresh parsley

1 tbsp chopped fresh thyme, plus extra sprigs to garnish

¾ cup heavy cream

salt and pepper

1 Melt the butter in a large saucepan over medium heat. Add the shallots and cook, stirring, for 3 minutes, until slightly softened. Add the leek and cook for another 5 minutes, stirring. Add the chicken, stock, and herbs. Season to taste with salt and pepper. Bring to a boil, then lower the heat and simmer for 25 minutes, or until the chicken is tender and cooked through. Remove from the heat and let cool for 10 minutes.

2 Transfer the soup to a food processor or blender and process until smooth. Return the soup to the rinsed-out pan and reheat gently over low heat.

3 Stir in the cream and cook for an additional 2 minutes, then remove from the heat and ladle into warmed bowls. Garnish with sprigs of thyme and serve immediately.

chicken & potato soup with bacon

SERVES 4

1 tbsp butter

2 garlic cloves, chopped

1 onion, sliced

9 oz/250 g smoked bacon, chopped

2 large leeks, sliced

2 tbsp all-purpose flour

4 cups chicken stock

1 lb 12 oz/800 g potatoes, chopped

7 oz/200 g skinless chicken breast, chopped

4 tbsp heavy cream

salt and pepper

grilled bacon and fresh flat-leaf parsley sprigs, to garnish

1 Melt the butter in a large saucepan over medium heat. Add the garlic and onion and cook, stirring, for 3 minutes, until slightly softened. Add the chopped bacon and leeks and cook for another 3 minutes, stirring.

2 In a bowl, mix the flour with enough stock to make a smooth paste and stir it into the pan. Cook, stirring, for 2 minutes. Pour in the remaining stock, then add the potatoes and chicken. Season to taste with salt and pepper. Bring to a boil, then lower the heat and simmer for 25 minutes, until the chicken and potatoes are tender and cooked through.

3 Stir in the cream and cook for another 2 minutes, then remove from the heat and ladle into warmed bowls. Garnish with the cooked bacon and flat-leaf parsley and serve immediately.

thai chicken-coconut soup

SERVES 4

4 oz/115 g dried vermicelli noodles

5 cups chicken or vegetable stock

1 lemongrass stalk, crushed

½-inch/1-cm piece fresh ginger, peeled and very finely chopped

2 fresh kaffir lime leaves, thinly sliced

1 fresh red chile, or to taste, seeded and thinly sliced

2 skinless, boneless chicken breasts, thinly sliced

scant 1 cup coconut cream

2 tbsp Thai fish sauce

1 tbsp fresh lime juice

scant ½ cup bean sprouts

4 scallions, green part only, finely sliced

fresh cilantro leaves, to garnish

1 Cook the dried noodles according to the package directions. Drain well and set aside.

2 Meanwhile, bring the stock to a boil in a large saucepan over high heat. Lower the heat, add the lemongrass, ginger, lime leaves, and chile and simmer for 5 minutes. Add the chicken and continue simmering for an additional 3 minutes, or until cooked. Stir in the coconut cream, fish sauce, and lime juice and continue simmering for 3 minutes. Add the bean sprouts and scallions and simmer for an additional 1 minute. Taste and gradually add extra fish sauce or lime juice, if needed. Remove and discard the lemongrass stalk.

3 Divide the noodles among warmed bowls. Bring the soup back to the boil, then remove from the heat and pour over the noodles (the heat of the soup will warm the noodles). Garnish with the cilantro and serve immediately.

chicken & lemon soup

SERVES 4

4 tbsp butter

8 shallots, thinly sliced

2 carrots, thinly sliced

2 celery stalks, thinly sliced

8 oz/225 g skinless, boneless chicken breasts, finely chopped

3 lemons

5 cups chicken stock

8 oz/225 g dried spaghetti, broken into small pieces

⅔ cup heavy cream

salt and pepper

2 lemon wedges, halved, to garnish

1 Melt the butter in a large saucepan. Add the shallots, carrots, celery, and chicken and cook over low heat, stirring occasionally, for 8 minutes.

2 Thinly pare the lemons and blanch the lemon rind in boiling water for 3 minutes. Squeeze the juice from the lemons.

3 Add the lemon rind and juice to the pan, together with the stock. Bring the soup slowly to a boil over low heat and let simmer for 40 minutes, stirring occasionally.

4 Add the spaghetti to the pan and cook for 15 minutes. Season to taste with salt and pepper and add the cream. Heat through, but do not let the soup boil, or it will curdle. Remove from the heat.

5 Ladle into warmed bowls and garnish with the lemon wedges. Serve immediately.

Step 1

Step 2

Step 3

chicken noodle soup

SERVES 4–6

2 skinless chicken breasts

5 cups water or chicken stock

3 carrots, cut into ¼-inch/ 5-mm slices

3 oz/85 g thin noodles

salt and pepper

fresh tarragon leaves, to garnish

1 Place the chicken breasts in a large saucepan, add the water, and bring to a simmer. Cook for 25–30 minutes, skimming off any foam that rises to the surface. Remove the chicken from the stock and keep warm.

2 Continue to simmer the stock, add the carrots and noodles, and cook for 4–5 minutes.

3 Thinly slice or shred the chicken breasts and place in warmed bowls.

4 Season the soup to taste with salt and pepper and pour over the chicken. Serve immediately garnished with the tarragon.

chinese chicken balls in broth

SERVES 6

8 cups chicken stock

3 oz/85 g shiitake mushrooms, thinly sliced

6 oz/175 g bok choy or other Chinese greens, sliced into thin ribbons

6 scallions, finely sliced

salt and pepper

chicken balls

1 oz/25 g chicken, minced

1 oz/25 g fresh spinach leaves, finely chopped

2 scallions, finely chopped

1 garlic clove, very finely chopped

pinch of Chinese 5-spice powder

1 tsp soy sauce

1 To make the chicken balls, put the chicken, spinach, scallions, and garlic in a bowl. Add the 5-spice powder and soy sauce and mix until combined.

2 Shape the chicken mixture into 24 meatballs. Place them in one layer in a steamer that will fit over the top of a saucepan.

3 Bring the stock just to a boil in a saucepan that will accommodate the steamer. Regulate the heat so that the liquid bubbles gently. Add the mushrooms to the stock and place the steamer, covered, on top of the pan. Steam for 10 minutes. Remove the steamer and set aside on a plate.

4 Add the bok choy and scallions to the pan and cook gently in the stock for 3–4 minutes, or until the leaves are wilted.

5 Divide the chicken meatballs evenly between warmed bowls and ladle the soup over them. Serve immediately.

chicken gumbo soup

SERVES 6

2 tbsp olive oil

4 tbsp all-purpose flour

1 onion, finely chopped

1 small green bell pepper, seeded and finely chopped

1 celery stalk, finely chopped

5 cups chicken stock

14 oz/400 g canned chopped tomatoes

3 garlic cloves, finely chopped or crushed

4½ oz/125 g okra, stems removed, cut into ¼-inch/5-mm thick slices

4 tbsp white rice

7 oz/200 g cooked chicken, cubed

4 oz/115 g cooked garlic sausage, sliced or cubed

salt and pepper

1 Heat the oil in a large, heavy saucepan over medium–low heat and stir in the flour. Cook for about 15 minutes, stirring occasionally, until the mixture is a rich golden brown.

2 Add the onion, green bell pepper, and celery and continue cooking for about 10 minutes, or until the onion softens.

3 Slowly pour in the stock and bring to a boil, stirring well and scraping the bottom of the pan to mix in the flour.

4 Add the tomatoes and garlic. Stir in the okra and rice and season to taste with salt and pepper. Reduce the heat, cover, and simmer for 20 minutes, or until the okra is tender.

5 Add the chicken and sausage and continue simmering for about 10 minutes. Remove from the heat, ladle into warmed bowls and serve immediately.

chicken & summer vegetable soup

SERVES 4

2 tbsp olive oil

2 skinless, boneless chicken breasts, thinly sliced

2 garlic cloves, peeled and crushed

2 zucchini, cut into ½-inch/1-cm dice

7 oz/200 g green beans, cut into ½-inch/1-cm pieces

12 oz/350 g tomatoes, seeded and coarsely chopped

14½ oz/410 g canned pinto or borlotti beans, drained and rinsed

5 cups vegetable stock

12 fresh basil leaves, torn into pieces

pepper

Parmesan cheese shavings, to serve

1 Heat the oil in a large saucepan set over medium heat. Add the chicken and garlic and cook, stirring, for 3 minutes. Try not to let the chicken or garlic brown.

2 Stir in the zucchini, green beans, tomatoes, pinto beans, and stock. Cover and simmer for 10–12 minutes, or until the chicken is cooked through and the vegetables are tender. Remove from the heat.

3 Stir in the basil leaves and season to taste with pepper. Ladle into warmed bowls and serve immediately with Parmesan cheese shavings.

Step 1

Step 2

Step 2

chicken & leek soup

SERVES 4–6

2 tbsp butter

12 oz/350 g boneless chicken, diced

12 oz/350 g leeks, cut into 1-inch/2.5-cm pieces

5 cups chicken stock

1 bouquet garni

8 pitted prunes, halved

scant 1 cup cooked rice

1 red bell pepper, seeded and diced (optional)

salt and white pepper

1 Melt the butter in a large saucepan. Add the chicken and leeks and cook for 8 minutes.

2 Add the chicken stock and bouquet garni to the pan and stir well. Season to taste with salt and pepper, bring to a boil, and let simmer for 45 minutes.

3 Add the prunes to the pan with the cooked rice and diced bell pepper (if using) and let simmer for 20 minutes.

4 Remove from the heat and remove and discard the bouquet garni. Ladle into warmed bowls and serve immediately.

curried chicken soup

SERVES 4–6

½ **cup butter**

2 onions, chopped

1 small turnip, cut into small dice

2 carrots, finely sliced

1 apple, peeled, cored, and chopped

2 tbsp mild curry powder

5 cups chicken stock

juice of ½ lemon

6 oz/175 g cold cooked chicken, cut into small pieces

2 tbsp chopped fresh cilantro, plus extra to garnish

salt and pepper

½ **cup cooked rice, to serve**

1 Melt the butter in a large saucepan over medium heat. Add the onions and sauté gently, until soft but not brown.

2 Add the turnip, carrots, and apple and continue to cook for an additional 3–4 minutes.

3 Stir in the curry powder until the vegetables are well coated, then pour in the stock. Bring to a boil, cover, and simmer for about 45 minutes. Season to taste with salt and pepper and add the lemon juice.

4 Transfer the soup to a food processor or blender. Process until smooth and return to the rinsed-out saucepan. Add the chicken and cilantro to the pan and reheat gently.

5 Remove the soup from the heat. Divide the rice between warmed bowls and ladle the soup over the top. Garnish with cilantro and serve immediately.

chicken & lentil soup

SERVES 6

3 tbsp olive oil

1 large onion, chopped

2 leeks, chopped

2 carrots, chopped

2 celery stalks, chopped

scant 2½ cups chopped white mushrooms

4 tbsp dry white wine

5 cups vegetable stock

1 bay leaf

2 tsp dried mixed herbs

¾ cup green lentils

scant 2½ cups diced cooked chicken

salt and pepper

1 Heat the oil in a large saucepan. Add the onion, leeks, carrots, celery, and mushrooms and cook over low heat, stirring occasionally, for 5–7 minutes, or until softened but not colored.

2 Increase the heat to medium, pour in the wine, and cook for 2–3 minutes, until the alcohol has evaporated. Pour in the vegetable stock. Bring to a boil, add the bay leaf and herbs, reduce the heat, cover, and simmer for 30 minutes.

3 Add the lentils, re-cover the pan, and simmer, stirring occasionally, for for an additional 40 minutes, or until they are tender.

4 Stir in the chicken, season to taste with salt and pepper, and simmer for another 5–10 minutes, until heated through. Remove from the heat and remove and discard the bay leaf. Ladle into warmed bowls and serve immediately.

chicken & mushroom soup with puff pastry

SERVES 4

2 chicken legs, skin removed

4 cups chicken or vegetable stock

⅔ cup hard cider

1 onion, finely chopped

1 bay leaf

3⅔ cups thickly sliced cremini mushrooms

4 tbsp cornstarch blended with 4 tbsp water

4 tbsp sour cream

about 1 lb 2 oz/500 g prepared puff pastry dough (depending on shape of soup bowls or mugs)

all-purpose flour, for sprinkling

salt and pepper

1 Put the chicken legs in a large saucepan with the stock, hard cider, onion, and bay leaf. Cover and simmer for 25 minutes. Add the mushrooms and simmer for 10 minutes. Remove the chicken and set aside. Remove and discard the bay leaf.

2 Stir the cornstarch mixture into the stock. Heat, stirring, until boiling and thickened. Remove from the heat and let cool. Remove the meat from the chicken legs and tear into pieces.

3 Preheat the oven to 400°F/200°C. Stir the chicken and sour cream into the soup. Season to taste with salt and pepper, then ladle into ovenproof bowls or mugs. They should be about three-quarters full.

4 Roll out the dough on a floured counter. Cut out rounds or squares large enough to cover the tops of the bowls with a ½-inch/1-cm overlap. Brush the rim of each bowl with water, lay the dough on top, press around the rim, and pierce the centers. Bake in the preheated oven for 20–25 minutes, or until the soup is bubbling hot and the pastry is golden.

Step 1

Step 1

Step 4

chicken, squash & spinach soup

1 tbsp butter

1 tbsp oil

3 skinless, boneless chicken breasts, about 4 oz/115 g each, cubed

2 small leeks, green parts included, thinly sliced

1 small butternut squash, peeled and cut into ¾-inch/2-cm cubes

1 small fresh green chile (optional), seeded and very finely chopped

14 oz/400 g canned chickpeas, drained and rinsed

¼ tsp ground cumin

4 cups chicken stock

2½ cups baby spinach leaves, coarsely chopped

salt and pepper

warm Italian bread, to serve

1 Melt the butter with the oil in a large saucepan over medium–low heat. Add the chicken, leeks, squash, and chile, if using. Cover and cook, stirring occasionally, for 10 minutes, or until the vegetables are beginning to soften.

2 Add the chickpeas and cumin and season to taste with salt and pepper.

3 Pour In the stock. Bring to a boil, then reduce the heat and simmer gently for 40 minutes, or until the squash is tender.

4 Stir in the spinach and cook for an additional 30 seconds, or until the spinach is just wilted. Remove from the heat.

5 Ladle into warmed bowls and serve immediately with warm Italian bread.

turkey soup with mushrooms & sage

SERVES 4–5

3 tbsp butter

1 onion, finely chopped

1 celery stalk, finely chopped

25 large fresh sage leaves, finely chopped

4 tbsp all-purpose flour

5 cups turkey or chicken stock

⅔ cup brown rice

9 oz/250 g mushrooms, sliced

7 oz/200 g cooked turkey, diced

¾ cup heavy cream

salt and pepper

sprigs of fresh sage, to garnish

freshly grated Parmesan cheese, to serve

1 Melt half the butter in a large saucepan over medium–low heat. Add the onion, celery, and sage, and cook for 3–4 minutes, or until the onion is softened, stirring frequently. Stir in the flour and continue cooking for 2 minutes.

2 Slowly add about one quarter of the stock and stir well, scraping the bottom of the pan to mix in the flour. Pour in the remaining stock, stirring to combine completely, and bring just to a boil.

3 Stir in the rice and season to taste with salt and pepper. Reduce the heat and simmer gently, partially covered, for about 30 minutes, or until the rice is just tender, stirring occasionally.

4 Meanwhile, melt the remaining butter in a large skillet over medium heat. Add the mushrooms and season to taste with salt and pepper. Cook for about 8 minutes, until they are golden brown, stirring occasionally at first, then more often after they start to color. Add the mushrooms to the soup.

5 Add the turkey to the soup and stir in the cream. Continue simmering for about 10 minutes, until heated through. Remove from the heat and ladle into warmed bowls. Garnish with sage and serve immediately with Parmesan cheese.

lemon turkey soup with mushrooms

SERVES 4

12 oz/350 g boneless turkey, cut into ½-inch/1-cm pieces

4 cups chicken stock

1 onion, quartered

2 carrots, thinly sliced

2 garlic cloves, halved

1 pared strip lemon rind

1 bay leaf

1 tbsp butter

12 oz/350 g small button mushrooms, quartered

4 tbsp cornstarch

½ cup heavy cream

freshly grated nutmeg

fresh lemon juice, to taste (optional)

1–2 tbsp chopped fresh parsley

salt and pepper

1 Put the turkey in a large saucepan and add the stock. Bring just to a boil, skimming off any foam that rises to the surface.

2 Add the onion, carrots, garlic, lemon rind, and bay leaf. Season to taste with salt and pepper. Reduce the heat and simmer, partially covered, for about 45 minutes, stirring occasionally, until the turkey is cooked.

3 Remove the turkey and carrots with a slotted spoon and reserve, covered. Strain the stock into a clean saucepan. Discard the onion, garlic, lemon rind, and bay leaf.

4 Melt the butter in a skillet over medium–high heat. Add the mushrooms, season to taste with salt and pepper, and cook gently until lightly golden. Reserve with the turkey and carrots.

5 Mix together the cornstarch and cream. Bring the cooking liquid just to a boil and whisk in the cream mixture. Boil very gently for 2–3 minutes until it thickens, whisking almost constantly.

6 Add the reserved meat and vegetables to the soup and simmer over low heat for about 5 minutes until heated through. Taste and adjust the seasoning, adding nutmeg and a squeeze of lemon juice, if using. Stir in the parsley. Remove from the heat and ladle into warmed bowls. Serve immediately.

provençal turkey soup

SERVES 4–5

1 tbsp olive oil

2 red, yellow, or green bell peppers, seeded and finely chopped

1 celery stalk, thinly sliced

1 large onion, finely chopped

½ cup dry white wine

14 oz/400 g canned plum tomatoes

3–4 garlic cloves, finely chopped

4 cups turkey or chicken stock

¼ tsp dried thyme

1 bay leaf

2 zucchini, finely diced

12 oz/350 g cooked diced turkey

salt and pepper

chopped fresh basil, to garnish

1 Heat the oil in a large saucepan over medium heat. Add the bell peppers, celery, and onion and cook for about 8 minutes until softened and just beginning to color.

2 Add the wine and simmer for 1 minute. Add the tomatoes and garlic.

3 Stir in the stock. Add the thyme and bay leaf, season with salt and pepper to taste, and bring to a boil. Reduce the heat, cover, and let simmer for about 25 minutes, or until the vegetables are tender.

4 Add the zucchini and turkey. Continue cooking for an additional 10–15 minutes, or until the zucchini are completely tender. Remove from the heat and remove and discard the bay leaf.

5 Ladle into warmed bowls, garnish with the basil, and serve immediately.

Step 1

Step 2

Step 4

turkey & lentil soup

SERVES 4

1 tbsp olive oil

1 garlic clove, chopped

1 large onion, chopped

7 oz/200 g mushrooms, sliced

1 red bell pepper, seeded and chopped

6 tomatoes, skinned, seeded, and chopped

generous 4 cups chicken stock

⅔ cup red wine

3 oz/85 g cauliflower florets

1 carrot, chopped

1 cup red lentils

12 oz/350 g cooked turkey meat, chopped

1 zucchini, chopped

1 tbsp chopped fresh basil

salt and pepper

thick slices of fresh Italian bread, to serve

1 Heat the oil in a large saucepan. Add the garlic and onion and cook over medium heat, stirring, for 3 minutes, or until slightly softened. Add the mushrooms, bell pepper, and tomatoes, and cook for an additional 5 minutes, stirring. Pour in the stock and red wine, then add the cauliflower, carrot, and red lentils. Season to taste with salt and pepper. Bring to a boil, then lower the heat and simmer for 25 minutes, or until the vegetables are tender and cooked through.

2 Add the turkey and zucchini to the pan and cook for 10 minutes. Stir in the basil and cook for an additional 5 minutes, then remove from the heat and ladle into warmed bowls. Serve immediately with slices of fresh Italian bread.

turkey & blue cheese soup

SERVES 4

4 tbsp butter

1 large onion, chopped

1 leek, sliced

11½ oz/325 g cooked turkey meat, sliced

2½ cups chicken stock

5½ oz/150 g blue cheese, crumbled

⅔ cup heavy cream

1 tbsp chopped fresh tarragon

pepper

fresh tarragon leaves and croutons, to garnish

1 Melt the butter in a saucepan over medium heat. Add the onion and cook, stirring, for 4 minutes, or until slightly softened. Add the leek and cook for another 3 minutes.

2 Add the turkey to the pan and pour in the stock. Bring to a boil, then reduce the heat and simmer gently, stirring occasionally, for about 15 minutes. Remove from the heat and let cool a little.

3 Transfer half of the soup to a food processor or blender and process until smooth. Return the mixture to the pan with the rest of the soup, stir in the blue cheese, cream, and tarragon and season to taste with pepper. Reheat gently, stirring. Ladle into warmed bowls and garnish with tarragon and croutons. Serve immediately.

chinese-style duck broth

SERVES 4–6

2 duck leg quarters, skinned

4 cups water

2½ cups chicken stock

1-inch/2.5-cm piece fresh ginger

1 large carrot, sliced

1 onion, sliced

1 leek, sliced

3 garlic cloves, crushed

1 tsp black peppercorns

2 tbsp soy sauce, or to taste

1 small carrot, cut into thin strips or slivers

1 small leek, cut into thin strips or slivers

3½ oz/100 g shiitake mushrooms, thinly sliced

1 oz/25 g watercress leaves

salt and pepper

1 Put the duck in a large saucepan with the water. Bring just to a boil, skimming off any foam that rises to the surface. Add the stock, ginger, carrot, onion, leek, garlic, peppercorns, and soy sauce. Reduce the heat and simmer, partially covered, for 1½ hours.

2 Remove the duck from the stock and set aside. When the duck is cool enough to handle, remove the meat from the bones and slice thinly or shred into bite-sized pieces, discarding any fat.

3 Strain the stock and press the vegetables with the back of a spoon to extract all the liquid. Remove as much fat as possible. Discard the vegetables and herbs.

4 Bring the stock just to a boil in a clean saucepan and add the strips of carrot and leek, the mushrooms, and duck meat. Reduce the heat and cook gently for 5 minutes, or until the carrot is just tender.

5 Stir in the watercress and continue simmering for 1–2 minutes until it is wilted. Taste the soup and adjust the seasoning if needed, adding a little more soy sauce, if desired. Remove from the heat and ladle into warmed bowls. Serve immediately.

duck soup with scallions

2 duck breasts, skin on

2 tbsp red curry paste

2 tbsp vegetable oil

bunch of scallions, chopped

2 garlic cloves, crushed

2-inch/5-cm piece fresh ginger, grated

2 carrots, thinly sliced

1 red bell pepper, seeded and cut into strips

4 cups chicken stock

2 tbsp sweet chili sauce

3–4 tbsp soy sauce

14 oz/400 g canned straw mushrooms, drained

1 Slash the skin of the duck 3–4 times with a sharp knife and rub in the curry paste. Cook the duck breasts, skin-side down, in a wok or skillet over high heat for 2–3 minutes. Turn over, reduce the heat and cook for a further 3–4 minutes, until cooked through. Lift out and slice thickly. Set aside and keep warm.

2 Meanwhile, heat the oil in a wok or large skillet over medium–high heat and stir-fry half the scallions, the garlic, ginger, carrots, and red bell pepper for 2–3 minutes. Pour in the stock and add the chili sauce, soy sauce, and mushrooms. Bring to a boil and simmer for 4–5 minutes. Remove from the heat.

3 Ladle the soup into warmed bowls, top with the duck slices, and garnish with the remaining scallions. Serve immediately.

VARIATION

If you don't like duck meat, replace the duck breasts with chicken breast pieces, skin-on.